The **OFFICIAL DVSA GUIDE** to
BETTER
DRIVING

Dr Lisa Dorn

Dr Lisa Dorn is an Associate Professor in Driver Behaviour and Director of the Driving Research Group at Cranfield University. She has edited 17 books and is an author on over 50 research papers.

Lisa is

- President of the International Association of Applied Psychology – Traffic and Transport Psychology Division
- Associate Fellow of the British Psychological Society
- a member of the Institute of Ergonomics and Human Factors.

As Research Director for DriverMetrics.com, Lisa has devised a 15-minute online assessment of behavioural risks, which produces a psychometric profile tailored to shed light on the behavioural risks associated with driving.

London: TSO

First published 2015
Second edition 2020

ISBN 978 0 11553967 1

A CIP catalogue record for this book is available from the British Library

Other titles in the Driving Skills series

The Official DVSA Theory Test for Car Drivers
The Official DVSA Theory Test for Car Drivers (DVD-ROM)
The Official DVSA Guide to Learning to Drive
The Official DVSA Guide to Hazard Perception (DVD-ROM)

The Official DVSA Theory Test Kit iPhone/Android App
The Official DVSA Highway Code iPhone App
The Official DVSA Hazard Perception Practice iPhone/Android App

The Official DVSA Guide to Riding – the essential skills
The Official DVSA Theory Test for Motorcyclists
The Official DVSA Theory Test for Motorcyclists (DVD-ROM)
The Official DVSA Guide to Learning to Ride
Better Biking – the official DVSA training aid (DVD)

The Official DVSA Guide to Driving Buses and Coaches
The Official DVSA Guide to Driving Goods Vehicles
The Official DVSA Theory Test for Drivers of Large Vehicles
The Official DVSA Theory Test for Drivers of Large Vehicles (DVD-ROM)
Driver CPC – the official DVSA guide for professional bus and coach drivers
Driver CPC – the official DVSA guide for professional goods vehicle drivers

The Official DVSA Guide to Tractor and Specialist Vehicle Driving Tests (eBook)
The Official DVSA Theory Test for Approved Driving Instructors (DVD-ROM)

Every effort has been made to ensure that the information contained in this publication is accurate at the time of going to press. The Stationery Office cannot be held responsible for any inaccuracies. Information in this book is for guidance only.

All metric and imperial conversions in this book are approximate.

DVSA wishes to thank Peter Rodger of IAM RoadSmart for his contributions, and gratefully acknowledges the input of all other reviewers.

We're turning over a new leaf.

RECYCLED
Paper made from
recycled material
FSC® C002151

Find us online

> GOV.UK – Simpler, clearer, faster

GOV.UK is the best place to find government services and information for

- car drivers
- motorcyclists
- driving licences
- driving and riding tests
- towing a caravan or trailer
- medical rules
- driving and riding for a living
- online services.

Visit **www.gov.uk** and try it out.

You can also find contact details for DVSA and other motoring agencies like DVLA at **www.gov.uk**

You'll notice that links to **GOV.UK**, the UK's central government site, don't always take you to a specific page. This is because this kind of site constantly adapts to what people really search for and so such static links would quickly go out of date. Try it out. Simply search what you need from your preferred search site or from **www.gov.uk** and you should find what you're looking for. You can give feedback to the Government Digital Service from the website.

Driver & Vehicle Standards Agency

The Driver and Vehicle Standards Agency (DVSA) is an executive agency of the Department for Transport.

We improve road safety in Great Britain by setting standards for driving and motorcycling, and making sure drivers, vehicle operators and MOT garages understand and follow roadworthiness standards. We also provide a range of licensing, testing, education and enforcement services.

www.gov.uk/dvsa

The Driver and Vehicle Agency (DVA) is an executive agency within the Department of the Environment for Northern Ireland.

Its primary aim is to promote and improve road safety through the advancement of driving standards and implementation of the government's policies for improving the mechanical standards of vehicles.

nidirect.gov.uk/motoring

⊙ Contents

⊕ Message from Mark Winn, the Chief Driving Examiner

In December 2017, we introduced changes to the test which were designed to make sure that new drivers have the skills they'll need to help them through a lifetime of safe driving.

Candidates now have to drive independently for a longer time in the test, and most will be asked to drive using a sat-nav. They have to demonstrate not just basic driving skills but also an understanding of the theory of driving and an ability to drive without instruction.

Good driving isn't just about control of the car and knowing the rules of the road – it's also about being a responsible driver and coping with the traffic situations you'll meet. Developing that responsibility comes, in part, with experience but it's also about your personal approach. For example, do you think you set a good example while you're driving – to your passengers (particularly children), and other road users?

We all start out knowing how to drive well – otherwise how would we have passed the test? We know that behaviours like using a mobile phone while driving and speeding aren't good. But bad habits can creep in. We may become over-confident – or lose confidence altogether; all of these things can increase our risk of crashing.

A good driver is just as aware of their faults as they are of their abilities, so you've scored on that measure by picking up this book. *Better Driving* explains how your attitude, mood, health and other factors can affect the way you behave at the wheel. We invite you to reflect on your style of driving and to consider how you can improve on that style.

We hope this book helps you to find your own unique way to be a better driver. You could be rewarded with lower costs, more confidence and enjoyment, and less stress. You'll also set a great example to your passengers and other road users. Most importantly, we hope it will help you towards a lifetime of safe driving.

Mark Winn

Mark Winn
Chief Driving Examiner for Great Britain
Driver and Vehicle Standards Agency

⊕ Introduction

You can improve your driving skills and hazard perception through practice under the guidance of an approved driving instructor (ADI). However, responsibility for improving your behavioural skills lies with you. This is because driving **skill** relates to your ability to manoeuvre your car safely in traffic, whereas your **behaviour** depends on psychological factors: it's an outcome of your lifestyle, personality, motivations and temperament.

This book will help you to understand yourself as a driver and give you the techniques you need to address your personal risk from a behavioural perspective. You'll not only become a better driver but also boost your confidence levels and increase your enjoyment of driving.

Driving skills vs driver behaviour – what's the difference?
It's important to understand the difference between 'driver behaviour' and 'driving skills'. Driver behaviour doesn't refer to the manual skills you need to drive your vehicle safely. Rather, it means the way you choose to use those driving skills in the traffic environment and your personality and emotional state when you come to drive.

Most incidents are the result of poor driver behaviour. Typical behaviours that increase risk include

- a bad decision by the driver – for example, going through traffic lights as they turn red
- not paying enough attention to what's going on around you
- unsafe speed choices
- not leaving enough space between your vehicle and other road users
- using a mobile phone while driving.

REMEMBER The way you behave as a driver is influenced by your thoughts and feelings.

Who is this book for?

This book will benefit all drivers, but it's especially relevant to

- those who are returning to driving after a break, to update you on the knowledge and skills you need to drive safely
- anyone looking to drive for their job, or increasing their mileage for work
- drivers who've recently been convicted of a traffic offence, to help you reflect on the reasons you committed the offence and work out how to improve your driving in the future
- nervous drivers looking to develop strategies to improve their confidence levels
- older drivers, to help you evaluate your driving and reduce your risk
- ADIs, as supporting material in your understanding of the human aspects of driving
- anyone interested in the psychological aspects of driving.

How is the book structured?

To help you get the most from the book, you'll find

Self-reflection boxes to get you thinking about your driving

Tips and strategies for safer driving

Science boxes to help you understand how you process information when you drive

Key information about driving and the law

There are also

FACTS boxes with important information to help you learn

REMEMBER boxes to help you keep essential tips and techniques in mind

Links to other resources

Definitions boxes to help explain important terms

In addition, you'll find

- evidence-based assessments to help you discover how your mind works and how this might affect your driving
- scenario-based learning, to help you understand how you typically respond in certain situations, and reflect on how you could improve
- diagrams and images.

Life-long learning

Many drivers assume that passing their driving test means they have the necessary knowledge and skills to drive through to old age, but there can be many challenges to overcome along the way. You may be reading this book because you're having some difficulties with your driving for one reason or another. You may not have driven for a while and need to get up to date with how to drive on today's roads. You may have particular concerns or simply want to learn something new to be a better driver.

Most people never receive any additional driver training after passing their driving test and may feel ill-equipped for today's roads. The good news is that this is nothing unusual – from time to time everyone feels the same. Safe driving is a life-long process of discovery and there's always something new to learn. Nobody can ever know everything, but the tools and techniques you'll find in this book will help you become a better and safer driver.

Section one

➡ The human factors in driving

In this section you'll learn

- about driving and your mental workload
- how thoughts, feelings and beliefs affect your behaviour at the wheel
- how to reflect on the way you drive
- about thrill-seeking tendencies and their effects on your driving
- how angry and stressed driving affects your safety
- how to deal with driving under pressure.

⊙ You, the driver

If you were to write down the most important factors in driver safety, what would be on your list? It's likely that you'd mention your skill as a driver, the rules of the road and the actions of other road users. You'd be right, too – all of these have a major influence on your driving. What you might not mention is the single most important factor of all: you, the driver.

The way you think about driving and the way you feel when you come to drive can be described as the 'human factors' in driver safety. Six of the main human factors that can affect your driving performance are

1. How you process information – how do your brain and eyes work while you're driving?

2. Your 'mental landscape' – how do your thoughts and feelings affect your driving decisions?

3. Risk perception – how do you assess road risk and how is this affected by your beliefs about what might happen?

4. Confidence – how does your belief in your ability and skills influence your driving decisions and risk taking?

5. Your personality – how do your thrill-seeking tendencies influence the way you drive?

6. Stress, mood and emotions – how do your feelings, including anger and nervousness, affect your ability to drive safely?

> Think about the questions in the list above. How would you answer them?

Defensive driving

Before we take a closer look at how human factors affect the way we drive, it's important to mention that becoming a better driver requires a defensive approach to driving. Defensive driving goes beyond the mechanics of handling a vehicle and understanding the rules of the road. Its aim is to reduce your risk of collision by anticipating potentially dangerous situations.

In particular, defensive driving involves

- awareness
- anticipation
- planning
- staying in control.

It also means driving with

- responsibility
- care
- consideration and courtesy.

This can be achieved by practising specific driving techniques that are covered in this book and in *The Official DVSA Guide to Driving – the essential skills*.

Defensive driving means reducing the dangers associated with driving, by heightening your awareness of everything that's happening around you. It means controlling the way you think and feel and not being negatively affected by the behaviour of other road users. As a defensive driver, you quickly identify potential problems on the road and immediately decide on the best course of action.

Take this approach to driving and you'll be a better and safer driver – particularly if you acknowledge that an element of risk is involved every time you get in a car.

⊕ How you process information

Most of the information that your brain processes while you're driving is visual. This includes

- information from the road environment
- other vehicles
- pedestrians
- road signs
- the scenery you're passing.

You may be processing information from other sources at the same time – for example, listening to music or talking with a passenger. You may also be thinking about where you're going or planning what you'll do once you arrive.

External and internal inputs like these bombard your brain with information. When you're driving, you must select the most important information to avoid making mistakes. There are simply not enough mental resources available to carry out all the tasks at the same time.

Driving is particularly difficult when

- the information flow becomes a torrent (for example, you're driving fast)
- the information is of low quality (for example, visibility is poor because you're driving at night or in bad weather)
- resources must be focused on a particular piece of information (for example, a hazard captures your attention)
- your mental capacity is reduced (for example, due to drugs, alcohol, stress or fatigue).

Most road traffic collisions happen when critical information was available but went unnoticed. For example, you may have failed to notice and act upon this information because your mental resources were focused elsewhere. In other words, you were distracted.

An imperfect system

The brain is a complex organ and can make mistakes when interpreting the world around us. Our eyes are able to capture only a small fraction of the visual information that's available, so the brain fills in the gaps and makes assumptions.

The way we process information is also extremely limited. We can only attend to a small amount of the information we

We can only attend to small amounts of the visual information we receive

receive, from which we make our decisions and respond. All the other information that's available either goes unnoticed or slips from memory.

There's always the possibility that we'll miss a hazard unless we look directly at it. Even then, there's no guarantee that we'll respond to it, as we often look but fail to see a hazard because the brain hasn't processed the potential for the hazard to unfold.

  Have you ever been at a junction, looked and not seen a cyclist or motorcyclist?

 For an example of how the brain selectively processes information, have a look at this video.

youtube.com/watch?v=vJG698U2Mvo

Once your brain has decided to take action – for example, to brake – it takes about three-quarters of a second for your body to react and move your foot from the accelerator to the brake pedal. You may travel up to 31 metres (100 feet) during that time, depending on your speed – and this assumes that your reaction times aren't impaired by other human factors, such as fatigue or the effects of alcohol.

 REMEMBER Don't forget the rule that thinking distance + braking distance = stopping distance. At 70 mph, you travel 31 metres (about three coach lengths) every second.

Thinking distance
(distance travelled in the time it takes to react to a situation)

 +

Braking distance
(distance travelled from when you start to use the brakes to when your car completely stops)

 =

Stopping distance

The science of hazard perception

The way the brain functions when anticipating the threat from developing hazards may be responsible for the difference in risk between an experienced driver and a novice driver.

Imagine you're driving and you suddenly notice a pedestrian stepping out in front of you. Even with just a hint of movement in your peripheral vision, your full attention is guided towards the hazard. Your brain doesn't waste time telling its 'thinking part' that the pedestrian is about to step into the path of your car and that you should brake.

Your visual cortex (the part of your brain that receives and processes what your eyes take in) feeds the information to the brainstem (the part of the brain that's attached to the spinal cord). This information is then sent on to the area of the brain that controls movement. At this point, your foot moves to touch the brake. This is an automatic response based on past experience. It's thought that our brain leaves a 'marker' whenever it encounters a threat, allowing it to respond more quickly when the same kind of scenario occurs again.

Why is this important? Well, there's evidence to suggest that this 'automated response' allows experienced drivers to react earlier to hazards. The process only seems to develop with repeated exposure to different hazards and road situations. This could explain why experienced drivers are better able to avoid risky situations than inexperienced drivers.

Information is processed here

Information

Reaction time 0.75 seconds

Hazard perception is a core driving skill. How many of these hazards would you have recognised if they weren't circled?

How good are your hazard perception skills?

How good do you think your hazard perception skills are? Studies have found that drivers have virtually no insight into how good they are at recognising and responding to hazards. In fact, these studies tell us that drivers often judge their hazard perception skills to be far better than they actually are. This may be due to the traffic environment being quite forgiving of the errors we make. In other words, when we fail to see a hazard, other road users can take avoiding action and compensate for our mistake.

To learn more about practising your hazard perception skills, visit the Official DVSA Learning Zone website and take a look at *The Official DVSA Guide to Hazard Perception Online*.

dvsalearningzone.co.uk/shop/hazard-perception

Distractions

With so many in-car gadgets, distraction is now even more of a problem for drivers. Most of us will have changed the radio station while driving and come through unscathed, so we may wonder whether the presence of these technologies really compromises our safety. Well, the **extent** to which a driver is distracted depends on the type of task, **when** it's performed and **how long** it takes to complete. Short tasks that require an easy response (such as pressing a button) don't demand much of the brain, but longer tasks that require a response to a menu (programming a sat-nav or using a mobile phone, for example) are **very** demanding and shouldn't be attempted on the move.

Keep your eyes on the road, not your phone.

THINK! road safety campaign poster showing the effects of distracted driving.

REMEMBER Don't allow any distraction, large or small, to compromise safety. (!)

Who gets distracted?

Younger, inexperienced drivers and older drivers are more vulnerable than others to the distracting effects of technology – but for different reasons.

- For young drivers, distraction is due to a greater inclination to engage in risk-taking behaviour, such as using a mobile phone while driving. This is because the risk of doing so isn't considered or recognised.

- For older drivers, distraction is more likely to be due to a decline in their visual and/or cognitive faculties (meaning anything that relates to mental processes, such as thinking, learning and remembering).

Strategies for dealing with distraction

Ask yourself

- Is there a safe place where you can stop and take stock?
- Do you really need to take that phone call?

Think about

- whether you can use alternative transport to go out with friends
- the type of music you're playing (see Section 2 for more information) and how loud it is. If the volume is too high, it might start to affect your driving.

Self-reflection scenario

You're on a night out with your friends and are now driving them home after midnight. They've been drinking and are arguing loudly.

Ask yourself

- How can you make sure that you get everyone home safely?
- What could you do to make sure your passengers don't distract you?

Strategies for safer driving

- Focus on the road, not on what's happening in the car.
- Ask your passengers to quieten down so you don't make any mistakes.
- Be confident enough to say you need to make sure everyone gets home safely.
- Talk to your passengers in a friendly way so you don't upset anyone.
- Tell them you need to concentrate – especially when driving in the dark.

Mental workload

Some driving tasks create a greater mental workload than others. Junctions can be particularly challenging in terms of the amount of information you have to process. At a junction you need to make a solid assessment of the speed and distance of oncoming vehicles, sometimes in both directions. You also need to look out for pedestrians and cyclists. Other vehicles may be queuing behind you and this may make you feel anxious, as you want to avoid keeping other road users waiting too long.

Ask yourself

- How long do you spend looking at junctions?
- Are you always sure that you've judged the speed and distance of oncoming traffic correctly?
- Have you checked for cyclists and motorcyclists?

You should make sure that you check the blind spots. Smaller vehicles take up less space in your visual field and might be overlooked.

Many collisions are caused by a failure to correctly judge the speed of oncoming vehicles or work out whether there's a sufficient gap to join the traffic on a main road. On average, drivers spend just 0.5 seconds visually searching at junctions.

REMEMBER Keeping on top of your ability to anticipate, detect and respond to hazards is a core skill for drivers.

⊛ Your mental landscape

As we saw in the introduction, there's a difference between 'driver behaviour' and 'driver skill'. Driver behaviour is influenced by motives, attitudes, emotional responses to traffic, personality traits, lifestyle, etc, whereas driver skill is related to your ability behind the wheel. This includes your knowledge of The Highway Code and your technical skills in manoeuvring the vehicle. It's possible to have excellent driving skills but very poor driving behaviour.

Driving is an activity that gives you a large element of control over how you interact with your vehicle and other road users. The main goal in driving is to reach a destination, but this ultimate goal comprises many other associated goals, such as reaching the destination quickly, comfortably, enjoyably and safely. In order to fulfil these goals, a wide range of tasks must be performed by you, the driver. You need to have the right mental skills to perform these tasks well.

Driving, thinking and feeling

The way you **think** and **feel** affects how well you drive. Your thoughts and feelings have an impact on how vulnerable you are to internal and external sources of distraction while driving. For example, feeling stressed about being late might make you more prone to mental distraction. Your thoughts and feelings also affect your hazard perception skills. For example, driving too fast because you think you're not at risk will mean that you're less able to perceive hazards, given the increased information flow.

> **REMEMBER** Your thoughts and feelings are reflected in your behaviour when you drive. Negative emotions, anger, anxiety and frustration can all compromise your safety and must be addressed if you're to become a better driver. ⓘ

What are you thinking?

Your beliefs or ways of thinking are fairly consistent patterns of thoughts or 'attitudes' that determine the way you interpret or make sense of what's going on around you and the behaviour of other road users. To become a safer and more confident driver, you need to understand the beliefs and thought patterns that underpin the way you drive.

> **REMEMBER** It's not the traffic events themselves that determine how you feel and act – it's the way you interpret and evaluate those events.

You may not be aware of the perceptions and expectations you hold. You may not have even questioned whether the way you think about other road users is valid. These 'hazards in the mind' can lead to intentional or unintentional risk taking. For example, you may believe that drivers who 'cut you up' are doing so deliberately. This way of thinking might lead you to drive faster or react angrily to a driver who does this, to teach them a lesson. Some road users may end up feeling intimidated to the point where they no longer wish to drive.

How are you feeling?

While you may not be consciously aware of the way you think and how this influences your driving behaviour, you can be consciously aware of how you feel when driving. You may find yourself acting on your feelings and expressing them behind the wheel without linking these feelings with your thought processes. Your feelings are an essential part of your decision making as a driver.

Consider the example of the driver cutting you up. Your way of thinking meant that you interpreted this as a hostile act, which then led to feelings of annoyance. If you think that other drivers should never cut you up (belief), you're likely to feel angry if they do (feelings). Feeling angry can affect your decision making by directing your attention exclusively towards the driver who broke your rule. Instantly, your brain tells you to retaliate. This can swamp your ability to process other critical information and, as a result, it increases your risk.

Assess your way of thinking and feeling

There's a clear link between your thought processes, your feelings and your behaviour. In order to discover this link, you need to reflect and gain insight into the way your mind works when you're driving.

Driver beliefs and feelings can take many forms. It's impossible to list them all, but you can ask yourself what some of your beliefs might be and how they affect the way you feel.

Our beliefs, feelings and driving behaviours are all connected.

Sometimes the way you feel as a driver can affect your thought processes. At the same time, the way you feel in response to driving-related events helps to develop your beliefs.

As an example of how this works in practice, think about a situation in your driving life that has made you feel very anxious. Can you identify what thought processes are underpinning your nervousness? What's at the root of your worries? Perhaps you **believe** you're not skilled enough to deal with, say, bad weather on a motorway? Perhaps you worry about large vehicles driving too close?

Once you've identified the way that your thought processes are affecting the way you feel, you can take action to change the way you look at different road and traffic situations. This will help to reduce your anxiety. More practical guidance on this can be found in Section 3.

You can also try to separate your thoughts and feelings from your driving skills. Ask yourself: if you weren't so nervous, would you be able to drive better? This will help you to identify whether you need to address your beliefs about your driving and increase your confidence or whether you genuinely need to improve your driving skills. In both circumstances, an approved driving instructor (ADI) can help you.

Self-reflection and driving ability

Feedback is critical to developing your driving. Imagine if your driving instructor didn't give you any feedback when you made mistakes during your driving lesson. Without your driving instructor correcting faulty decisions, you could easily develop bad habits and drive in a way that puts you and other road users at risk.

You need to develop your self-awareness and provide feedback to yourself throughout your driving life. Being able to reflect on your thought processes and your emotional reactions to driving will provide that feedback and help you to improve.

Self-reflection scenario

The last time you took your car out, someone drove too close behind you and sounded their horn to get you to move out of the way. They overtook you and you could see they were shouting at you as they passed by at speed. You felt very annoyed at the time and you were distracted from driving for a few minutes afterwards as you thought about what happened.

To self-reflect, start by replaying this scenario in your head, but this time really focus on your thoughts and feelings while you were driving.

- What was it about this situation that made you feel annoyed? Was it because of the increased risk in the situation? Was it because you felt the other driver was out of order? There might be a number of other reasons but only you can answer this question.

- Once you know what was at the root of your anger, you'll understand yourself better.

- By understanding what makes you angry, you have more control over how you choose to respond.

- You can choose to make sure the behaviour of other road users doesn't distract you from driving safely.

Triggers for self-reflection

To become better drivers, we have to recognise the triggers that tell us it's time for self-reflection. Broadly, triggers for self-reflection occur when you're surprised by another driver's actions or find yourself getting angry or nervous.

Think about the last time you got annoyed with another driver, then consider the following questions.

- What was the point of your journey?
- Were you in a hurry?
- What was going on in your mind before you got annoyed?
- Were you already in a bad mood?
- Did you think that this particular road user wasn't following the rules of the road?
- Is it realistic to expect all road users to follow the traffic rules all the time?
- How did it make you feel when the other driver failed to do things properly?
- Was it useful to get annoyed because of the other driver's actions?
- Were you already feeling under pressure before the event took place?
- Did you drive close to the other driver to teach them a lesson or make aggressive gestures? If so, how did your response increase the risk of an incident taking place?
- Looking back, what could you have done differently to reduce any risk in that situation?
- How can you make more of an allowance for other road users' mistakes next time?

If your thoughts, feelings and beliefs have such an effect on the way you drive, is there any way you can deal with negative responses to certain situations? The answer is yes, because driver behaviour is primarily learned. This means that faulty beliefs can be challenged through self-reflection.

This questionnaire will help you to self-analyse.

safedrivingforlife.info/self-reflection-survey

Next steps

- Through self-reflection, develop a strategy for how to reduce your risk in the future.
- Think about how you could make safer decisions next time.

⊕ Risk perception

One of the human factors that can have a strong impact on the way you choose to drive is how you perceive risk.

There are surprisingly few collisions on the road, considering how much traffic there is. In fact, your chances of being involved in an incident on any one trip are close to zero. Unfortunately, if you rarely see a collision, this can lead you to believe that it isn't always necessary to follow the rules of the road.

If you believe there's little chance that you'll have a crash, then you're more likely to take risks and increase your statistical risk by the way you choose to drive. Driving too quickly will increase your risk relative to other road users.

On the other hand, if you believe you're highly likely to be involved in an incident, then your perception of risk is much greater. You'd be more likely to drive with extreme caution to avoid what you judge to be the inevitable crash.

It's clear that there are strong individual differences in our perception of risk, with some people underestimating and others overestimating the risk. This belief in your chances of being involved in an incident has an important effect on your behaviour, so it's worth considering in more detail.

Your driving safety bubble

Some researchers believe that, on a day-to-day basis, drivers rarely think about risk at all. Instead, they maintain space around their car at a level they're comfortable with. (This is often referred to as the personal safety margin.) Driving soon becomes an unconscious habitual activity based on maintaining this safety bubble.

Some drivers' safety bubbles are too small. These drivers tend to enter other people's safety bubbles – for example, by travelling too close to the vehicle in front. This makes other drivers feel uncomfortable and, worse still, increases the risk of incidents.

In this diagram, the red car has entered the white car's safety bubble. This is because the driver of the red car has an incorrect perception of the 'safe distance' from the car in front.

Optimism bias

Optimism bias is a kind of distortion in the way you perceive risk. It causes you to believe that you're less at risk of being involved in an incident than other drivers. It's a general belief that leads you into thinking that you can expect to have a more positive experience of driving than others. The danger with this way of thinking is that you may not follow the rules of the road if you think you're not going to be involved in an incident in the first place.

While young drivers as a group are more likely to drive dangerously and be involved in road traffic collisions, not all young drivers have an optimistic bias and high-risk tendencies. Some young drivers have a strong aversion to risk and consider that their risk of being involved in a crash is high. You may hold a pessimistic bias that a negative event is highly likely to happen to you. This way of thinking can lead to anxiety, which can affect your driving performance in different ways.

Think about it. How big is your safety bubble?

How close do you drive to vehicles in front of you? How close are you prepared to drive to vehicles alongside you? What if you needed to brake sharply? Could you stop in time?

How optimistic are you about your driving experiences?

You're driving on a dual carriageway in heavy traffic. The traffic is preventing you from driving as fast as you'd like to drive. Generally, you like to be driving at around the speed limit of the road you're on. You're just a couple of metres from the car in front and staring blankly ahead. Suddenly, the line of traffic comes to a complete standstill and you narrowly avoid going into the back of the car in front.

Ask yourself

- How could you avoid this scenario in the future?
- Think about your habit of driving at the speed limit of the road you're on. How could you prepare better for unexpected events?
- In which situations are you most likely to drive without being properly aware of what's going on?

Strategies for safer driving

- Review your perception of risk in this situation – was it over-optimistic for the circumstances?
- Stay aware of the dangers of driving 'on automatic pilot'.
- Be aware of the brake lights on vehicles ahead of you to allow for a smooth reaction. Braking should be progressive – in other words, steadily increased, not sudden.
- Follow the 'two-second rule' and leave a safe gap.
- Make sure you allow larger gaps in bad weather and when driving at night to allow for longer braking times and poorer visibility.
- Look around and through the windows of the vehicles ahead of you, as far as the road horizon, to check for brake lights coming on further up the line of traffic. This will help you to anticipate what action might be required in good time.
- Look in your mirrors and scan to the sides frequently.
- You may need to move your head and body or slightly alter your car's position to get a better look.
- Check your speed regularly – it's very easy to increase your speed without realising it, and this will close the gap between you and the vehicle ahead.

As drivers we are relatively poor at estimating risk, for a number of reasons

1. You get little feedback on your risk taking because risky behaviours can be performed regularly with no consequences. This is because forgiveness for errors and violations is built into the traffic system. (See Section 4 for more about how vehicle and road engineering has helped to improve road safety.) Other road users can often take avoiding action when you do something wrong. It's only when a certain combination of factors occurs that an incident takes place. A collision is often the result of the actions of more than one party and you may not be prepared to accept blame for your own actions. We have a strong human tendency to blame other road users and fail to acknowledge the role we played in an incident.

2. Also, our capacity to recall risky experiences, such as near misses is poor. As a result, you're unlikely to learn from your mistakes and will have a tendency to repeat them.

3. You tend to believe you're more likely to experience a positive event than a negative one (optimism bias).

You can use this understanding of the way we all perceive risk to be a better driver.

Test yourself

What do you think are your chances of being involved in a collision in the next 12 months?

0   1   2   3   4   5   6   7   8   9   10

not at all   very likely

Compared with other drivers, how likely do you think it is that you'll be involved in a collision in the next 12 months?

0   1   2   3   4   5   6   7   8   9   10

not at all   very likely

19

Where did you place yourself? Typically, you'll have shown some optimism bias if you believe you're safer than the average driver in your peer group (ie people of the same age and sex as you). If you estimated your own risk of collision in the next 12 months to be lower than that of your peer group, then you've shown that you may be vulnerable to this way of thinking – like many road users.

Whether your self-rating is realistic or unrealistic is difficult to determine, but most drivers judge themselves to have less than a 10% probability of being involved in a crash. If you're a new driver, your actual risk is around 20% in the first year of driving. If you rated your risk as much higher than this – in other words, you think you're very likely to be involved in a crash – then perhaps you need to question whether your confidence levels are too low or whether you need to develop your driving skills, or both.

Next steps

- Look again at the rating you gave yourself. Consider whether your self-assessed probability of being involved in a collision is optimistic. Have you underestimated your risk?
- If there's a big difference between your rating of your own risk and your rating of the risk for other drivers, ask yourself whether this difference is realistic. Is your driving really that much better than other people's?

⊕ Confidence

Newly licensed drivers often become overconfident in their abilities soon after passing their driving test, despite their lack of experience. For example, studies of novice drivers have shown that they're inclined to be excessively confident in their ability to predict the behaviour of other road users. This makes them feel justified in taking risks such as speeding or tailgating. Novice drivers also tend to believe they can control the traffic situation to a greater extent than is realistic given the amount of driving experience they have.

How skilful a driver are you?

Have a look at the following table and estimate how much skill you have in each of the following aspects of driving. Use this scale:

0 – Well below average
1 – Below average
2 – About average
3 – Above average
4 – Well above average

	Below average		Aver-age	Above average	
	0	1	2	3	4
Management of your car in heavy traffic					
Performance in a critical situation					
Hazard perception in traffic					
Driving in a strange city					
Keeping to the traffic rules					
Managing the car through a skid					
Predicting traffic situations ahead					
Driving carefully					

	Below average		Aver-age	Above average	
	0	1	2	3	4
Knowing how to act in particular traffic situations					
Fluent lane-changing in heavy traffic					
Fast reactions					
Making firm decisions					
Paying attention to other road users					
Driving fast if necessary					
Driving in the dark					
Controlling the vehicle					
Avoiding competition in traffic					
Keeping sufficient following distance					
Adjusting your speed to the conditions					
Overtaking					
Keeping to the speed limits					

	Below average		Aver-age	Above average	
	0	1	2	3	4
Avoiding unnecessary risks					
Tolerating other drivers' mistakes calmly					
Obeying the traffic lights					

How did you score?

You may have scored yourself highly in some of these areas and perhaps not so highly in others. Look carefully at those areas where you've scored yourself as above average. Are you sure your skills are above average all the time? Are there circumstances under which you're less likely to perform these driving tasks competently? Perhaps you might rate yourself differently when you're in a hurry or in a bad mood?

Whatever your perception of your driving skills, there's often a difference between what you think about your driving and your actual skills. Don't worry, it's not specific to individuals – this disconnect is due to a number of human biases in the way we think. In particular, we have a tendency to misperceive the way traffic events unfold and process information in our favour. These biases might be due to a number of different human factors

1. the tendency to ignore times when you weren't driving well
2. a self-serving selection of examples when your driving was skilful
3. the tendency to see what you expect to see
4. the way you were feeling at the time
5. your personality
6. your motivations while driving.

If you rated yourself poorly on driving skills, scoring yourself as below average, an ADI could help you improve both your skills and your confidence.

Understand your driving weaknesses

- Biases in your beliefs about your driving skills are a common human tendency we're mostly unaware of. The first step towards better driving is to acknowledge how biased your view of your driving skills might be.

  The next time another driver is aggressive towards you for making a mistake, instead of automatically defending your actions, consider what element of your driving needs to be improved. For example

  - Were you driving too close?
  - Did you force another driver to brake harshly?
  - Were you driving too fast for the conditions?
  - Did you fail to look in your mirrors and see this road user?

- Improve your driving skills by learning from your mistakes. For example, if you have a near miss after emerging from a junction, the next time you're in that situation, spend longer scanning the road for potential hazards before you move out.

Influencing your mental demands

We all make mistakes when driving. No matter how experienced you are or how well you've been trained, you can still get it wrong. Most drivers try to avoid overloading their ability to process information by regulating the way they drive. You can influence the demands on you as a driver by adjusting your actions.

For example, the faster you drive, the less time you have to process information, to make decisions, to take action and to correct errors – all of which makes your drive more difficult. Multitasking and other distractions, such as talking on a mobile phone (even if it's hands-free) or using a music system, make things even harder.

On the other hand, if you drive at an appropriate speed for the road you're on, you have more time to process information and make safe decisions.

Errors, lapses and violations

Even the best drivers make mistakes, do foolish things or bend the rules at one time or another. Some of these behaviours are trivial, but others are potentially dangerous. Look at each of the following items and think about how often you've done these kinds of things over the past year. Make a mental note of how often you commit errors, lapses and violations.

Error – when we have a plan about how we intend to make a manoeuvre but execute it ineffectively

Lapse – usually due to a failure in your concentration

Violation – a deliberate action that breaks the law.

Attempt to overtake someone you hadn't noticed to be signalling a right turn	**ERROR**
Get into the wrong lane when approaching a roundabout or a junction	**LAPSE**
Miss 'stop' or 'give way' signs and narrowly avoid colliding with traffic having right of way	**ERROR**
Misread the signs and leave a roundabout on the wrong road	**LAPSE**
Fail to notice that pedestrians are crossing when turning into a side street from a main road	**ERROR**
Drive especially close to the car in front as a signal to its driver to go faster or get out of the way	**VIOLATION**
Forget where you left your car in a car park	**LAPSE**
Queuing to turn left onto a main road, you pay such close attention to the main stream of traffic that you nearly hit the car in front	**ERROR**
When reversing, hit something that you hadn't previously seen	**LAPSE**

Cross a junction knowing that the traffic lights have already turned against you	**VIOLATION**
On turning left, nearly hit a cyclist who has come up on your inside	**ERROR**
Disregard the speed limits late at night or very early in the morning	**VIOLATION**
Attempt to drive away from the traffic lights in third gear	**LAPSE**
Fail to check your rear-view mirror before pulling out, changing lanes, etc	**ERROR**
Have a dislike for a particular class of road user, and show your hostility in any way you can	**VIOLATION**
Become impatient with a slow driver in the outer lane and overtake on the inside	**VIOLATION**
Underestimate the speed of an oncoming vehicle when overtaking	**ERROR**
Switch on one thing, such as the headlights, when you meant to switch on something else, such as the windscreen wipers	**LAPSE**
Brake too quickly on a slippery road, or steer the wrong way in a skid	**ERROR**
Intending to drive to destination A, you 'wake up' to find yourself on the road to destination B, perhaps because B is your more usual destination	**LAPSE**
Drive even though you realise you may be over the legal blood-alcohol limit	**VIOLATION**
Get involved in unofficial 'races' with other drivers	**VIOLATION**
Realise that you have no clear recollection of the road you've just been travelling along	**LAPSE**
Angered by another driver's behaviour, you give chase with the intention of giving him/her a piece of your mind	**VIOLATION**

How did you score?

Look carefully at those areas that apply to you most often.

If you assessed yourself honestly, you'll know that thinking about why you've made a mistake is the first step towards finding out how you can avoid making the same mistake again.

Don't overthink and dwell on your mistakes, though. Learn from them and decide to become a better driver.

Ask yourself: under what circumstances am I more likely to commit errors, lapses and violations? Every time you make a mistake or commit a violation, there's an opportunity to be a better driver by reflecting on the reasons why it happened. These are the triggers for self-reflection discussed earlier in this section.

The ability to self-reflect on personal weaknesses, such as overconfidence in driving skills, is a core skill for all drivers. This is the first step towards acknowledging your weaknesses – which aren't necessarily due to poor driving skills, but may instead be due to the belief that your driving skills are above average and that you can therefore afford to take risks. Once you understand how your beliefs about risk and your confidence in your driving skills might influence your driving behaviour, the next step is to recognise this tendency when you're making decisions behind the wheel.

Next steps

- Reflect on the areas where you consider your skills to be above average. Are they realistic?
- Think about the errors, lapses and violations you're likely to commit. For example
    - Perhaps you have a tendency to drive too close to other vehicles in a traffic queue and might go into the back of another car?
    - Perhaps you have a tendency to drive too fast for the circumstances and may lose control of your car?
    - Perhaps you have a tendency to emerge from junctions without looking out for fast-moving vehicles in the far distance?

Once you've thought about these different kinds of scenarios, it's easy to discover how to reduce your risk.

⊙ Your personality

Sensation-seeking and thrill-seeking tendencies are personality characteristics with strong links to risk-taking behaviour. That might seem like a difficult thing to get your head around, but it's not quite as complex as it sounds.

'Sensation seeking' is the tendency to look for varied, novel, complex and intense sensations and a willingness to take risks for the sake of experiencing them. For example, that might include playing dangerous sports or using drugs.

'Thrill seeking' is the way in which sensation-seeking tendencies are expressed. On the road, that might mean speeding on unsuitable roads or making risky overtaking manoeuvres.

Thrill-seeking tendencies lead to risk taking, and risk taking increases your chances of being involved in a collision. For example, driving under the influence of alcohol is strongly associated with thrill-seeking tendencies.

FACTS

- Drivers in their 20s have the highest rates of drink-driving crashes.
- Young drivers who crash are twice as likely to be impaired by alcohol as older drivers who crash, and this is far more common among young men than among young women.

Test yourself

Are you a thrill-seeking driver? If you are, you can reduce your chances of being involved in a collision. Have a look at the following questionnaire and answer the questions as honestly as you can.

Thrill-seeking questionnaire
Answer the following questions on the basis of your usual or typical feelings about driving.

1. I get a buzz from the whole driving experience

0	1	2	3	4	5	6	7	8	9	10

not at all   very much

2. Safety is less important than the thrill of driving fast

0	1	2	3	4	5	6	7	8	9	10

not at all   very much

3. I get a thrill out of driving fast

0	1	2	3	4	5	6	7	8	9	10

not at all   very much

4. I like to raise my adrenaline levels while driving

0	1	2	3	4	5	6	7	8	9	10

not at all   very much

5. Being a racing driver would be a dream come true

0	1	2	3	4	5	6	7	8	9	10

not at all   very much

6. I sometimes like to frighten myself a little when driving

0	1	2	3	4	5	6	7	8	9	10

not at all   very much

7. I don't like having to slow down for a corner

0	1	2	3	4	5	6	7	8	9	10

not at all   very much

8. I would love to drive a sports car on a road with no speed limit

0	1	2	3	4	5	6	7	8	9	10

not at all   very much

9. I feel in control when I'm driving fast

0	1	2	3	4	5	6	7	8	9	10

not at all   very much

10. I enjoy the sensation of accelerating rapidly

0	1	2	3	4	5	6	7	8	9	10

not at all   very much

Your results

Add up your score and read the relevant category below to find out more about your thrill-seeking tendencies.

Routine driver (score between 0 and 25)
You prefer a well-ordered and routine style of driving and like to stick to the road rules. You have a traditional view of what driving should be about. For you, driving isn't about gaining excitement and enjoying the risks, but taking a steady, calm and structured approach in order to arrive safely.

Low-risk driver (score between 26 and 50)
You tend not to use driving as a source of excitement: you see it more as a way of getting from A to B than as a way to get your adrenaline rush for the day. You usually avoid taking corners at speed or driving fast when there are only a few cars on the road. You generally follow the rules of the road.

Occasional risk taker (score between 51 and 75)
You sometimes enjoy an adrenaline rush when driving fast and taking corners sharply. From time to time you might like to experience a buzz from driving, especially on open country roads with bends and hills. You sometimes like to accelerate rapidly and may ignore the road rules occasionally.

High-risk driver (score between 76 and 100)
You love the thrill of driving and are likely to take risks to raise your adrenaline levels, such as cornering at high speeds and accelerating rapidly. You enjoy creating an element of risk and you feel alive when you can experience the freedom of the open road at speed. Your thrill-seeking tendencies increase the chances of you being involved in a collision.

Think about your driving, especially when you have a near miss. There may be situations that make you feel excited and enjoy taking risks, especially on open country roads with bends and hills where you may feel like putting your foot down and cornering at speed. Remember that severe crashes are more likely to happen on rural roads.

Find out more about driving on country roads at this website.

https://think.gov.uk/road-safety-laws/#country-roads

And watch these videos.

https://think.gov.uk/campaigns/?filters=.country-roads

Next steps

- Reflect on how your personality affects the way you drive. Do you have a tendency to try to impress others with your driving or gain excitement through driving?

- Remember that accelerating rapidly may mean that other road users are unable to predict what you're going to do next. Try to remain aware of this and drive defensively.

- Resisting the urge to speed can make driving more enjoyable and give you a greater sense of control.

- Consider whether you drive differently when driving alone or with particular types of passenger. Try to recognise this tendency and take steps to drive safely no matter who is (or isn't) in the car with you.

- Think about the consequences of being involved in a crash and the effects it would have on your friends and family.

- Recognise the triggers that make you drive in a way that increases your risk of being involved in an incident. Are you more likely to take risks when you're under time pressure? Are you more likely to take risks when you're annoyed or tired?

⊕ Stress, mood and emotions

The association between stress and involvement in road traffic incidents is well established. Studies have found that people who have experienced recent traumatic life events (for example, divorce) have a greater risk of crash involvement.

There are thought to be two main reasons for this link

- Drivers who are stressed may be distracted by thoughts about their personal problems.

- Stress may cause drivers to lack the necessary motivation to avoid hazardous driving situations.

It has been estimated that drivers who have experienced stressful events such as personal conflicts, illness, bereavement or financial difficulties are five times as likely to cause fatal crashes as drivers who haven't been subjected to such stressful events.

People react to stress in different ways. Some drivers may experience high levels of stress even in routine driving conditions, whereas others remain calm and untroubled during the most difficult traffic environments and situations.

REMEMBER If you have anxiety or depressive illness that affects your memory or concentration, disturbs your behaviour or gives you suicidal thoughts, you should seek medical advice before driving. You might also need to notify the Driver and Vehicle Licensing Agency.

Road layout and driver stress

The road layout itself is an important aspect of the environment that can affect the way you drive. For example, junctions with poor visibility are dangerous because of the difficulty of hazard detection, but you may reduce your personal safety and the safety of other drivers if you overreact by worrying excessively about the problem.

On the other hand, feeling some risk while driving may help to reduce the likelihood that you'll become overconfident and underestimate your chances of being involved in an incident. It may also help you to develop safe coping strategies such as looking carefully before you emerge from a junction.

What kind of road layout do you find most difficult? For example, roundabouts, rural roads, motorways, etc.

Consider the link between road layout and your personality when driving. For example, do you put your foot down and enjoy the feelings of speed and exhilaration when you're confronted with an apparently empty road?

Are there certain kinds of road layout that trigger a reaction in you?

Time pressure

Driving under time pressure often leads to high-risk behaviour such as speeding and dangerous overtaking. This is particularly true for people who drive for work or those who have a busy schedule. The pressure may be due to your employer imposing strict deadlines or it may be a perceived time pressure that you place on yourself.

Not being able to reach a destination by a certain time only creates a problem if missing that time leads to some kind of penalty. In many situations there's no particular punishment for being late, apart from inconvenience, and you can remove the perceived pressure by calling ahead from a safe place with the engine switched off.

Heavy traffic earlier on your journey means you're late for an important appointment or to make a delivery.

Ask yourself

- Are the few minutes you might save really worth the risks you're tempted to take by driving too fast?
- What are the true consequences of lateness? Will being late really affect your employer's business?
- Can you pull over and call ahead to let the customer know you're running late due to heavy traffic?
- Would your employer or customer really want you to increase the risk of an incident and its consequences for yourself, other road users and the vehicle?

Improving your coping strategies

When you're driving under time pressure, you may use ineffective coping strategies that not only fail to deal with the stress but also create more risk for you and other road users.

A better coping strategy would be to

- plan your journey in advance
- give yourself as much time as possible by leaving early
- avoid travelling at busy times whenever you possibly can
- recognise how the stress of being under time pressure might affect your driving
- take some slow, deep breaths. Deep, controlled breathing stimulates the parasympathetic nervous system – the part of your nervous system that helps you to relax.

Other good coping strategies include

- being extra-vigilant when you know you're feeling stressed. Switch your attention from thinking about the source of stress to concentrating on the driving task

- focusing entirely on your driving. After all, arriving at your destination unharmed is the most important thing.

Think about how your driving differs when you're under time pressure.

Do you often find yourself running late and wishing you'd organised things better?

Are you more likely to take risks when you're running late?

Self-reflection scenario

You're driving on a country road on the way to visit a friend. You're running a little late and try to make up time by driving faster.

Ask yourself

- What's going through your mind? Are you thinking more about the consequences of being late than the consequences of having a crash?

- Have you taken into account the dangers of driving too fast on country roads?

- How much time are you really likely to save by driving a few miles an hour over the speed limit?

- Will it really matter if you're a few minutes late?

Strategies for safer driving

- Remember that you have ultimate control over how you choose to drive.

- Try not to create additional pressure by worrying about being late. Remember that the only pressure is the pressure you place on yourself.

- Pull over in a safe place, switch the engine off and phone your friend to let them know you're going to be a little late.

- Take it easy and enjoy the drive. You'll then arrive feeling relaxed and happy to see your friend, rather than stressed and irritated.

Angry driving

Angry drivers frequently express their irritation by behaving aggressively towards other road users. This can include

- verbal abuse
- gestures
- flashing lights
- tailgating
- horn blowing
- lane hogging.

Not surprisingly, such behaviour is known to be dangerous. Angry drivers may spend less time assessing situations and are quicker to allocate blame to others.

> Anger while driving is linked to negative views about other road users and often leads to intimidation tactics. These include behaviours such as tailgating, risky overtaking or trying to teach other road users a lesson.

Moods and angry driving

Your mood can change quickly in response to

- what's going on in your life
- traffic situations
- other road users.

Driving in a bad mood

- changes your driving style
- impairs driving performance
- increases your risk.

Angry driving impairs hazard perception

It's important to realise how much influence a bad mood can have on your ability to detect and respond to hazards. To be a safe driver, you need to be able to 'search' the road environment for developing situations. Feelings of frustration, anger or impatience may lead to a failure to detect developing hazards in your peripheral vision and may lead you to spend more time looking at certain hazards than responding to others. This is because strong emotions such as anger tend to take up a lot of your brain's processing capacity, leaving less for you to concentrate on your driving.

Self-reflection scenario

You're driving in the city at rush hour when someone pulls out right in front of you and you have to brake sharply. You're very annoyed and use your horn. You shout at the driver, who looks quite nervous and holds up their hand to apologise. You then accelerate sharply around the driver and continue on your way. You can feel the tension in your body.

Ask yourself

- What was going through your mind? Did you think that the driver deliberately pulled out in front of you?

- What if the driver was distracted and made a mistake? Would that change how you reacted?

- Have **you** ever made a mistake while driving?

- Does getting annoyed help the situation or change anything for the better?

- How did your reaction increase your risk?

Strategies for safer driving

- Try to give other drivers the benefit of the doubt. Remember that in most cases they don't deliberately set out to annoy you.

- Recognise that getting annoyed will only make the situation worse, by putting you at risk.

- Reframe the incident in a more positive way: instead of focusing on the other person's error, take pride in the way you were able to react to the hazard and avoid a collision.

- Choose to change the way you think about other road users who make a mistake. After all, we all make mistakes sometimes.

Test yourself

Driving these days is stressful, and all drivers get frustrated or angry in traffic from time to time. Think about how angry each of the following traffic situations would typically make you feel.

	Not at all angry	A little angry	Fairly angry	Very angry	Extremely angry
Someone in front of you doesn't move off straight away when the traffic lights turn green					
Someone is driving too fast for the road conditions					
A pedestrian walks slowly across the middle of the street, slowing you down					
Someone is driving too slowly in the outside lane and holding up traffic					
Someone is driving very close to your rear bumper					

	Not at all angry	A little angry	Fairly angry	Very angry	Extremely angry
Someone is weaving in and out of the traffic					
Someone cuts in right in front of you on the motorway					
Someone cuts in and takes the parking spot you've been waiting for					
Someone fails to indicate before turning off					
Someone is driving more slowly than is reasonable for the traffic flow					
A slow vehicle on a winding road won't pull over and let people pass					

	Not at all angry	A little angry	Fairly angry	Very angry	Extremely angry
You see a police car watching traffic from a hidden position					
Someone backs out right in front of you without looking					
Someone goes through a red light or 'stop' sign					
Someone beeps their horn at you about your driving					
Someone coming towards you doesn't dip their headlights at night					
At night, someone drives right behind you with their headlights on full beam					

	Not at all angry	A little angry	Fairly angry	Very angry	Extremely angry
You spot a speed camera site ahead					
Someone is slow to park and holds up traffic					
Someone speeds up as you try to pass them					
You're stuck in a traffic jam					
Someone pulls out right in front of you when there's no-one behind you					
Someone makes an obscene gesture towards you about your driving					
Someone is driving well above the speed limit					

	Not at all angry	A little angry	Fairly angry	Very angry	Extremely angry
Someone shouts at you about your driving					
A cyclist is riding in the middle of the lane, slowing down the traffic					
A police officer pulls you over					

Reflect on the driving situations that make you lose your temper and ask yourself what you can do to reduce your stress levels. Finding different strategies to tackle frustrations in traffic often makes you feel more in control and less prone to angry outbursts.

For example, it's highly unlikely that the driver in front of you who keeps braking sharply is deliberately trying to provoke you; they may just be lost. Remember that you have the power to change the way you think about this situation. Understanding your own triggers for outbursts is the first step towards controlling your feelings and increasing your tolerance of other road users and traffic situations.

⊕ Summary

In this section you've

- learned about the limitations on our mental capacity to process information
- looked at the way your thoughts and feelings affect your driving decisions
- considered how your level of confidence in your abilities influences the way you drive
- reflected on your personality characteristics and discovered whether you're a thrill-seeking driver
- learned how angry and stressed driving can compromise your safety.

As you can see, no single human factor predicts risky driving. Risky driving is likely to involve a complex set of circumstances and interactions between several different elements

1. your perceived level of risk, driving abilities, stress, mood, fatigue, personality, etc
2. your personal experiences as a driver: how long ago you passed your driving test, the amount of training you've received, your driving record, etc
3. situational factors: having passengers in the car, the purpose of the journey, etc
4. your chances of being caught and punished for committing a driving offence on your journey
5. non-human factors that will determine the level of risk for individual journeys, such as
   - the objective level of risk – for example the casualty rates on the road you're driving on
   - other factors you can't necessarily control, such as the time of day or the weather.

How can you drive better?

- Use the self-reflection exercise below before you drive.
- Make sure that you're aware of your cognitive and emotional state before, during and after your journey.

- Outside of work time, driving is usually an activity you can do at your own pace. You have a large amount of control over several elements that directly influence the way you drive; for example
  - when to begin your journey
  - what vehicle to use
  - which roads to take.

Before you start driving, ask yourself the following questions. If the answer to any of them is 'yes', don't drive until you're safe to do so.

- Are you angry, stressed or upset about anything? Might this impair your ability to drive defensively?
- Are you in a bad mood? Are you distracted by things that are going on in your life?
- Are you under time pressure?

- Program your sat-nav before you start your journey.
- Select the route you prefer and think about traffic congestion and times of day. This can help you to avoid delays and save fuel.
- Position your sat-nav so that it doesn't obstruct your vision but you can still glance at it easily when necessary.

- Make sure that your sat-nav doesn't obstruct an airbag.
- Stay alert to road signs, as you would if you weren't using the sat-nav.
- Don't rely on your sat-nav alone, as you may have set the destination incorrectly. You should also make sure that the maps in your sat-nav are up to date before you plan your journey.

In-car entertainment systems

Many people use in-car entertainment systems to listen to music or watch DVDs. These systems can be a major source of distraction for drivers because

- adjusting radios, CD players or MP3 players diverts your attention away from the road
- sound from passengers' DVD, laptop or tablet devices can affect your concentration.

Some drivers believe that music helps them to stay awake. However, one of the major disadvantages from a safety perspective is that fine-tuning radio controls and scrolling through playlists means that your attention is diverted from driving to adjusting the device.

You should **never** use DVD players or personal computers while you're driving.

- Set up a car playlist so that you don't need to adjust your music while you're driving. Make sure it's long enough for your journey.

- Pre-set your radio controls before you set off. Changing them on the move could be dangerously distracting.

- Keep the volume at a reasonable level. Loud music can reduce your ability to notice or react to hazards.

- In particular, make sure your music isn't so loud that you can't hear warning sounds from your vehicle or external warnings (horns and emergency sirens).

- Be careful not to get too 'drawn in' to the music in your car. This, too, can distract you from what's happening outside and affect your ability to respond to hazards.

- Be aware of the type of music you listen to while driving. In general, research suggests that up-tempo beats can cause you to increase your acceleration and take more risks, while slower-paced music may improve your driving behaviour.

Passengers

Passengers can also be distracting – especially for young and novice drivers. Responsible passengers will observe you as you drive and adapt their conversation and behaviour accordingly.

If you find that passengers are distracting your attention from your driving, either

- stop the vehicle in a car park, lay-by or service area and continue your conversation there, or

- tell them that your concentration is being affected.

Children

Children can be a major source of distraction, particularly if they're tired, hungry or bored by the journey.

In a study of journeys with rear-seat child occupants, children accounted for 12% of all potential sources of driver distraction. Over 75% of parent drivers were found to be turning around or using the rear-view mirror to look at their children, 16% engaged in conversation and a further 7% assisted their children by passing food and drink, etc. Drivers with children in the car were also significantly more likely to have their eyes off the forward roadway for more than two seconds while the vehicle was in motion.

- Try to keep children entertained by packing snacks, drinks and games along with you, so their attention is focused on something else. However, don't give the goodies out as you're driving; either stop somewhere safe or put them in a place where the children can easily access them without distracting you from the road.

- Consider playing them films or TV shows on mobile devices. Just be mindful of the sound level, in case it affects your concentration.

- If you're on a long journey, make sure you schedule regular comfort and exercise breaks.

Food and drink

Eating at the wheel can lead to a loss of concentration and often means you have only partial control of your vehicle.

- If you're going on a long journey, make sure you eat before you leave.

- Schedule regular stops to eat, drink and go to the toilet.

- Drink plenty of water to avoid dehydration, as this can negatively affect your concentration.
- Stop in a safe place before you take a drink.

Distracted driving and the law

In the UK, courts have the authority to decide whether **any** distraction (not just a mobile phone call) was a key contributory factor in a collision and made the driver negligent in their responsibility towards other road users. The introduction of new laws on causing death by careless and inconsiderate driving has opened the door for drivers to be prosecuted and potentially imprisoned for any form of distracted driving that results in a fatality.

Self-reflection scenario

You're driving a long way and are keeping yourself entertained by listening to some music. You don't want to listen to some of the tracks and keep skipping to find the ones you like. Now you decide to change the artist you're listening to and start scrolling through the list to find the one you want.

Ask yourself
- What could you do to make sure you stay focused on your driving?
- Is there anything you could do before you set off to minimise the risk of being distracted?

Strategies for safer driving
- Decide before your journey starts what kind of music you want to listen to.
- Set up your in-car entertainment system in advance to minimise your levels of distraction.
- Choose a reasonable volume level and make sure you can hear internal and external warning sounds.
- If you need to change your music, pull over in a safe place to do so.

⊕ Fatigue

Fatigue means feeling tired, sleepy or lacking in energy.

People tend to think of driver fatigue as something that's only experienced by long-haul lorry drivers and others who regularly spend long hours in a vehicle, but it affects us all.

Driver fatigue – the facts

Your driving performance can be affected by factors such as

- the time of day you're driving
- how long you've been awake before you start driving
- how long you spend driving on a particular journey
- the road environment.

Being a drowsy driver means you're

- three times as likely to be involved in a collision or near miss
- at risk of being involved in the 16% of all collisions (more than 20% on motorways) that happen as a result of sleepiness.

Remember

- Your body is naturally tired between the hours of 2 am and 7 am, and between 2 pm and 4 pm, with major peaks in risk at 3 am and 3 pm. Your chances of having a fatigue-related crash increase by six times when driving between the hours of midnight and 6 am.

- If you drive after being awake for 18 hours, your driving is comparable to that of a drunk driver.

- Your fatigue-related risk strongly increases when you've been driving for more than two hours.

- Fatigue sets in more quickly on some roads than on others. Motorways, for example, tend to be monotonous, with little visual stimulation to keep you alert. Roads such as these tend to make you feel tired.

How does fatigue affect your driving performance?

When you're fatigued, it

- affects your ability to scan for hazards
- impairs your judgement of speed
- makes it harder for you to maintain a straight path.

It can also have an impact on your reaction time; if a hazard unfolds suddenly, you're poorly equipped to react and avoid a collision.

It isn't clear whether this kind of impairment is due to a driver being so tired that they lack the motivation to drive safely, or whether they fail to monitor their driving performance as they grow more tired.

The effects of fatigue can strike quickly, particularly among drivers with underlying health issues or lifestyle factors that increase their likelihood of becoming fatigued. Many medications can increase drowsiness. Additionally, health problems such as sleep apnoea can cause fatigue. Sleep apnoea is when, during sleep, your breathing stops for short periods of time, affecting the quality of your sleep. This can lead to 'microsleeps' during the day, or when you're supposed to be awake. A microsleep is when you actually fall asleep for a moment, often without even realising it. As with mobile phone use, fatigue can be used to determine driver negligence in the event of an incident, and it can result in a criminal conviction.

If you're tired before you start your journey, or become fatigued during a long drive, how does it affect your driving? Are your reactions slower? Do you tend to use your mirrors less? Do you drift out of your lane and become more erratic in your speed choices?

How can you reduce your risk of a fatigue-related crash?

The increase in risk brought about by driving when you're tired means that it's vital to make sure you're well rested before a long journey. You should also plan regular rest breaks.

Stop and rest

When you're tired, the quality of your driving can degrade to such an extent that the only way to deal with it is to stop as soon as it's safe and legal to do so. If you're on a motorway, pull in at the nearest service area or leave at the next junction. The only time you're

allowed to stop on the hard shoulder of a motorway is in an emergency, so you **MUST NOT** stop there to rest.

If it isn't possible to stop immediately, open a window for fresh air. Then stop as soon as it's safe and legal to do so.

Caffeine

The most effective ways to counter sleepiness are caffeine and a short nap. The combination of a caffeinated drink (for example, caffeinated coffee) and a short nap of up to 15 minutes is particularly effective. Caffeine takes 20–30 minutes to act on the brain, giving you the opportunity for a nap. However, this shouldn't be used as a regular solution to your sleepiness.

What do you do to reduce your fatigue while driving? How can you plan your journey to include breaks and maintain your alertness?

- Get plenty of sleep (at least six hours) the night before driving, especially if it's a long trip.
- Share the driving with someone else if you can.
- Travel at times when you're normally awake.
- Stop driving if you become sleepy.
- Stay overnight in a hotel rather than drive while tired.
- Schedule a break every two hours or every 100 miles.
- Avoid working all day and then driving a long distance.
- Find a safe place to take a short nap.
- Travel with a passenger who's awake and alert.

⊛ Alcohol and drugs

Drink-driving

Since the breathalyser laws were introduced in 1967, there have been constant efforts to reinforce the message about the risks of drink-driving. These campaigns have largely been successful. However, while the number of alcohol-related crashes and drink-drive convictions has reduced, it remains a problem. The total number of casualties for drink-drive accidents was 8,700 in 2018. There has been an overall reduction in drink-drive fatalities in the last few decades, but this is mainly attributable to improvements in car and road safety. The most important factor is still the state of the driver.

FACTS

The drink-drive limit specified in law for England, Wales and Northern Ireland is

- 35 microgrammes of alcohol per 100 millilitres of breath
- 80 milligrammes of alcohol per 100 millilitres of blood
- 107 milligrammes of alcohol per 100 millilitres of urine.

In Scotland the law is different

- 22 microgrammes of alcohol per 100 millilitres of breath
- 50 milligrammes of alcohol per 100 millilitres of blood
- 67 milligrammes of alcohol per 100 millilitres of urine.

It's a criminal offence to fail to provide a specimen for analysis when required to do so by a police officer.

What plans do you make before drinking alcohol to ensure you don't drive while over the limit? Do you know how long the alcohol will stay in your system? Have you ever taken a chance, hoping you won't get caught?

REMEMBER The law doesn't cover Northern Ireland but you could still be arrested there if you're unfit to drive.

Find out more about drug-driving by watching these videos.

youtube.com/watch?v=Bz0tnwiYv4w#t=20

https://think.gov.uk/campaign/breathalyser-for-drugs/

Some medication leaflets and packaging state 'Do not operate heavy machinery'. A vehicle is a piece of heavy machinery, but it's such an integral part of day-to-day life that people tend not to view it as such. It's important to understand that the impaired driving is the illegal act, regardless of the legality of the drug or its source.

Do you check leaflets and avoid driving as recommended when taking medication?

Do you ask your doctor or pharmacist for advice about driving and taking medication?

Can you nominate a driver to help you to get around if you're taking medication?

- If in doubt about the effects medicines might be having on your driving ability, don't drive until you have all the information you need.

- Don't stop taking your medicines, prescribed or otherwise, but do talk to your doctor or ask your pharmacist for information.

To find out which health conditions or medical treatments you may need to tell DVLA about, visit this website.

www.gov.uk/driving-medical-conditions

⊙ New technologies

Vehicle engineering has seen significant advances in the past 30 years, with the introduction of improved safety measures such as

- inertia-reel seat belts
- airbags
- child restraints
- anti-lock braking systems (ABS)
- electronic stability control (ESC)
- independent vehicle safety testing – European New Car Assessment Programme (Euro NCAP).

Vehicle manufacturers have also invested heavily in the research and development of technology that

- helps a driver to avoid collision
- protects the occupants of a vehicle as much as possible in the event of a collision.

Remember your first car. How different was the interior of that vehicle from your present vehicle?

How have you adapted to changes in the vehicles you've driven over the years?

Vehicle engineering and behavioural adaptation

Sometimes, improvements in vehicle safety can have a negative effect on the way that people drive. A notable example is ABS, a technology designed to help drivers stop efficiently.

A project called the Munich taxi driver study looked at the behavioural impact of the introduction of ABS. Researchers studied collision rates and observed the driving behaviour of taxi drivers with and without ABS fitted in their cabs. They found there was no significant difference in their collision rates – in fact, the rate for drivers of ABS-equipped vehicles was slightly higher than the rate for those without ABS.

Human responses to technology aren't always straightforward. The Munich study revealed that the drivers with ABS-equipped vehicles braked harder, cornered more sharply, left less space in front of them, and failed to maintain lane positioning and merge with other traffic in a safe manner. This was likely to be due to the drivers **feeling** safer and therefore taking more risks.

> **REMEMBER** Advanced safety features can't protect you if you become complacent and take more risks.

> Have you noticed whether the technology in your vehicle has led to a change in the way you drive? Do you feel safer and therefore take more risks?
>
> Do you drive differently in new or hired vehicles that you know have state-of-the-art safety systems and gadgets?

For the past three weeks you've been driving a new company car that has cruise control. You really like being able to keep to a fixed speed so you can take your foot off the accelerator and let the car drive at the speed you've selected. It's been particularly useful on long, boring motorway journeys.

However, on your last motorway journey you suddenly had to brake sharply to stop your car ploughing into the back of a line of stationary traffic, which had stopped for roadworks up ahead. This was the first time in ages that you'd had to stop so quickly to avoid a collision and you wonder whether the technology has had an impact on your driving.

Ask yourself

- How can you make sure you stay focused on the primary task of driving, even when using in-vehicle technology?

- What can you do to make sure your ability to respond to hazards is just as sharp when you're using in-vehicle technology?

Strategies for safer driving

- Technology is there to reduce your workload so that you're able to drive safely. Be aware that when workload levels are really low, your attention might start to drift.

- Stay alert when using new technology by consciously maintaining control of the vehicle, in the same way as you would when driving without the technology.

- Make sure you don't rely on technology to get you out of trouble. Ultimately, you must be in control of the vehicle.

- Don't be tempted to drive at higher speeds than normal because of in-vehicle technology.

- Driving at a fixed speed is inappropriate in many traffic situations. Assess the traffic regularly and cancel cruise control in good time.

- Keep scanning the road ahead and checking your mirrors to maintain your hazard perception skills when using cruise control.

Positive and negative effects

Sometimes in-car technology can have both positive and negative effects on driver safety.

Positive

Sat-nav systems can help drivers to find their way around and avoid the worry and distraction caused by getting lost. They're particularly useful in challenging situations such as complex junctions or when unexpected diversions or road conditions make signs more difficult to follow. This means that drivers can concentrate on monitoring the constantly changing traffic situation for hazards, and making safer decisions, rather than focusing on finding the correct route.

Negative

It's easy to become over-reliant on in-car technology and allow it to make all the decisions. Most of us will have heard the stories about people who followed the directions on their sat-navs, only to find themselves travelling the wrong way down one-way streets or driving down railway lines! In these situations, the drivers may have become 'passive' and placed too much trust in the navigation system, rather than actively observing road signs or planning their journeys in advance. This means that something that's meant to help is often given a much higher level of control than may be safe.

How can you make sure that you always stay focused on your driving – allowing the technology to support you, rather than allowing it to take control?

How can you make sure you're prepared for potential hazards and changing circumstances?

Vehicle control systems

Sophisticated vehicle control systems are becoming more and more widespread. These systems are able to take full control of the vehicle if the on-board computer decides that it's necessary to do so. These systems include

- collision avoidance systems, which warn you of a possible collision and then take steps to apply braking on your behalf

- adaptive cruise control – an advanced version of cruise control that reduces your speed automatically when necessary, so that you always stay a safe distance from the vehicle in front

- intelligent parking assistance, which allows the vehicle to park itself if the conditions are right.

The safety value of some of these systems isn't yet clear, because they haven't been in production long enough to monitor their long-term effects on incident reduction.

Does your vehicle have collision avoidance systems?

Six of the most common new technologies are

- forward collision warning
- auto brake
- lane departure warning
- lane departure prevention
- adaptive headlights
- blind-spot detection.

Do you fully understand how your collision avoidance system works?

- A wide variety of driver assistance systems are available in cars these days. Make sure you read your vehicle's manual to fully understand how they work before they take you by surprise when you're driving.

- Don't rely on technology to let you know about an imminent collision. Stay focused and in control of the vehicle at all times and let the technology assist you instead.

⊕ The road environment

The UK road network has been engineered to work efficiently with the vehicles it carries and to give drivers as much information as possible to help them make safe decisions. Road engineering has also provided a physical environment that's designed to minimise the risk of serious injury or death when incidents do happen.

Innovations in road engineering through the years have included

- traffic lights
- roundabouts
- consistent warning signs
- effective and widespread safety barriers
- street lighting
- improvements to visibility at dangerous junctions
- wider roads
- converting crossroads into mini-roundabouts or intersections with signals
- traffic-calming measures in residential areas.

However, some researchers believe that driver behaviour adapts to changes in road engineering in the same way as it adapts to changes in vehicle engineering. In other words, as was found in the Munich taxi driver study, when drivers feel safer, some of them will take more risks. When roads have been widened, for example, some drivers have chosen to increase their speed because they think the road is safer.

Have you noticed whether your driving changes when you're on a well-engineered road? Think about a newly built road you've driven on, with fresh tarmac and no potholes. Or perhaps it's a widened road with clearer road signs. Do you feel that these roads are safer and therefore drive differently?

Engineering for behaviour

More recently, we've seen local innovations such as 'shared space' (also known as 'naked roads') in parts of the UK.

Shared space is a kind of street design that has

- minimal road markings
- few signs.

The theory is that reducing or removing the usual markings encourages road users to look around and decide who should have priority of movement.

You can find shared space in London, Brighton, Caernarfon and Ashford, as well as other parts of the UK.

Have you ever found yourself in a shared-space zone?

How have you made your way through unmarked or unsigned areas and taken the needs of other road users into equal consideration?

⊕ Summary

In this section you've

- considered the effects of distractions and fatigue on road safety
- looked in more detail at impaired driving and seen how alcohol and drugs can affect your driving ability
- learned how developments in vehicle technology and the road environment can affect your behaviour as a driver.

The road environment is constantly changing. Technological developments, engineering initiatives and new laws all have an influence on the way we drive. Our roads are safer than they've ever been, but you can help to make them even safer by understanding your own driving behaviour and the way you interact with your vehicle and the road.

Section three

⊙ Developing better strategies

In this section you'll learn

- about anxiety and driver ability
- some general tips for a less stressful drive
- how to deal with challenging driving scenarios
- strategies to help you stay on the right side of the law
- ways to adjust and reassess your driving as you get older
- how to improve your reaction to stressful situations.

→ Feeling nervous about driving

You might think that feeling nervous about driving is something that only happens to you, but you'd be wrong. Many drivers experience situations that make them feel anxious, nervous or confused. This could lead them to avoid certain journeys or, in extreme cases, any kind of driving activity at all. It goes without saying that neither of these outcomes is desirable. In both scenarios, a lack of confidence can affect your enjoyment of the social and professional opportunities that a vehicle can provide.

There are many reasons why you might feel nervous about driving. For example

- You may have learned to drive a long time ago but not driven for the past few years. You may not have the confidence to return to driving after such a long gap.

- You may put too much pressure on yourself to be a perfect driver and worry about the mistakes you might make.

- You may have recently been involved in a road traffic collision or near-miss, or been convicted of a traffic offence, and are now questioning your driving abilities.

- You may be going through a particularly stressful time in your life, such as changes to your financial or domestic situation, and this may be affecting how you feel. These feelings can be a serious distraction when driving.

- You may have lost confidence in your driving because someone has criticised you.

- You may have recently passed your driving test and feel that your skills aren't sufficient to cope with certain situations.

- You may feel there are too many demands on you as a driver. Perhaps you're noticing the effects of ageing, such as slower reaction times. Or perhaps you have a medical and/or physical condition – such as diabetes or arthritis – that's affecting your confidence in driving.

- You may have recently become a parent for the first time. The extra responsibility this brings may have caused you to become nervous about driving with the baby in the car.

If any of these sound familiar, then this section will give you a number of tools and techniques to help you enjoy your driving life again. Whatever the reasons for a decline in your self-belief, you'll be able to overcome your concerns and return to driving with confidence.

Which scenarios make you feel nervous?

Some drivers are anxious about particular types of road or road features, such as motorways, roundabouts or junctions. Others are anxious about particular traffic situations, such as

- when other vehicles, particularly large goods vehicles, are driving too close behind them
- driving in congested urban conditions or during the rush hour
- driving at night or in bad weather.

What makes you most nervous when you're driving?

How does being nervous affect your driving?

You may worry that the demands of driving are greater than your ability to cope with them. That's where effective coping strategies can help.

Anxiety and driving ability

Feeling anxious about driving has a negative effect on your driving performance, and makes you more likely to make a mistake. This is because you become distracted, worrying about what **might** happen instead of focusing on what you actually need to do. Reducing your anxiety levels will help you to concentrate on your driving, and therefore you'll be more likely to enjoy the experience.

Stress: brain, body and mind

When you feel anxious, physiological changes take place in your brain and body. These changes can have a big effect on your driving.

In normal, relatively mild fear reactions, such as those experienced by a nervous motorist, key neurons throughout the brain fire more rapidly, sending information around the brain and body, and creating a general state of anxiety. Perspiration levels, breathing rates and muscle tension increase. Being anxious can have a negative effect on your ability to process information about hazards and can increase your chances of missing important information. When you make a mistake or do something wrong, this heightens your state of anxiety, worry or fear. With repeated experiences over the long term, there may even be a downward spiral that leads you to give up driving altogether.

The kind of personality we have can determine how we respond to stress. The good news is that you can develop the characteristics of individuals who cope better with stress by using the strategies covered in this section. Such 'hardy' individuals believe that they can influence events and have control over their lives. They take responsibility for their own actions and respond flexibly to challenges as they arise. Hardy individuals view challenges as a normal part of everyday life and see them as an opportunity for growth and development. They're more likely to welcome challenges and not see them as a threat or try to avoid them.

General strategies for a less stressful drive

The following strategies will help you to stay safe, feel less stressed and get more enjoyment from your driving.

- Choose a route that places fewer demands on you, such as a road you're familiar with.
- Allow more time for your journey.
- Avoid driving at busy times (where possible).
- Avoid driving in bad weather.
- Focus on the task of driving. If you're distracted by worries or concerns, you should find a safe place to stop and only carry on driving when you can do so safely. Try not to let your worries or concerns about driving affect your concentration.
- Avoid being distracted by your mobile phone. Switch it off before you start driving.
- Reduce your mental workload by reducing your speed. The faster you drive, the more information you need to process.
- Find a quiet place to practise manoeuvres that might cause you stress, such as three-point turns in tight streets or parallel parking.
- Find an approved driving instructor (ADI) and ask for some additional training to top up your driving skills.

⊙ Coping with challenging scenarios

Have a look at the following scenarios and think about how you usually approach the situations they describe. Once you've read through them, take a look at the coping strategies underneath each one. How do they differ from your normal approach?

Use the scenarios in this section to develop your self-reflection toolkit: think about additional scenarios that are particularly relevant to you. Go through the steps to develop your self-awareness and the strategies you'll need to improve your driving.

Junctions

You're about to emerge from a junction and are feeling worried about the volume of traffic on the main road. You've been waiting a little while for a safe gap in the traffic and now there's a queue of vehicles behind you. You're starting to feel anxious about holding up the traffic. You think 'I must try and move out soon'.

You look in the rear-view mirror and the driver behind you is very close; you're afraid they might start sounding their horn to get you to move out when you're not ready. You can feel your anxiety levels rising.

Ask yourself

- How can you stay calm when you think other road users may be getting frustrated with you?
- What can you do to make sure you make safe decisions even under pressure?

Strategies for safer driving

- Remember that **you** are in charge of your vehicle and the decisions you make. Other road users mustn't influence you. Don't let yourself be intimidated into taking risks.

- Remind yourself that having to wait for a safe gap is due to the busy traffic and is no reflection on your driving skills. It may take time to judge the speed of the traffic, but this is a critical part of knowing when it's safe to go.

- Don't be distracted by what the drivers behind you might be thinking. You can't know what's going on in their minds. Concentrate on making a sensible assessment of the situation in front of you.

- If your view to the left or right is obstructed, you'll need to take some action to improve it, such as slowly edging forward.

- Remind yourself that there will eventually be a safe gap in the traffic. You won't be at this junction forever. Only go when you feel it's safe.

- Let other drivers deal with their own situation while you deal with your situation. They should be able to understand how busy the traffic is when it's their turn.

Roundabouts

You feel worried about pulling out on to a roundabout and being in the correct lane to exit. Sometimes you wait a long time to pull out. Other vehicles come round the roundabout so fast and they don't always indicate to let you know whether they're continuing round or turning off. Sometimes it feels like they're coming from all directions.

Ask yourself

- How can you approach a roundabout without feeling overwhelmed?

- What can you do to cope better with the demands of using roundabouts?

Strategies for safer driving

- Take some lessons with an ADI and get additional practice at driving on roundabouts. Practice makes perfect.

- Tell yourself that you can do this. After all, you've done it many times before.

- Take slow, deep breaths if you feel your anxiety levels rising.

- Check the road signs as you approach the roundabout. Plan how you need to approach, enter, drive around and exit the roundabout. Your plan will vary according to the design of the roundabout and your destination, but it should allow you to deal with the task safely.

- If you're on a spiral roundabout, remember that the lines spiral outwards from the centre of the roundabout and each lane has a designated exit. Road markings are used to keep vehicles in the correct lane, and to guide them towards the appropriate exit. You should comply with any signs, traffic lights and lane markings, and indicate only to change lanes as part of the normal mirror–signal–manoeuvre routine (see rule 133 of The Highway Code). You can find out more about spiral roundabouts in *The Official DVSA Guide to Driving – the essential skills.*

Strategies for safer driving

- Avoid turning around in your seat to check on your child, as this will take your attention away from the road.
- Avoid looking in the rear-view mirror at your child too often, as you need to concentrate on the road.
- Tell yourself that your child is safely strapped in and there's no need for concern. You'll soon be home.
- As soon as they're old enough to understand, start teaching your child about how they can help you to be a safer driver by being quiet.
- To reduce the chances that your child will complain about being hungry, give them a healthy snack before you set off.
- Play their favourite audio book or songs.
- On long trips, take regular breaks and make sure children have something to keep them amused – a few books, a tablet, an in-car DVD player or some favourite small toys.
- Make getting there part of the fun – for example, watching out for a familiar landmark (such as a church spire) that means they're nearly home.

REMEMBER If there's an emergency, pull over in a safe place before you help your child.

Driving at night

You need to make a trip after dark, but you're worried that the glare from vehicle headlights might dazzle you. You're concerned about your ability to see hazards properly and even about getting lost in the dark. You remember how difficult it is to manoeuvre your car into the tight spot in the car park. It will be even more difficult at night.

Ask yourself

- What can you do before driving at night to make sure you're as safe as possible?
- Once you're on the road, what can you do to maximise your safety?

Strategies for safer driving

- Certain types of glasses may be unsuitable for night driving, so check with your optician.
- Check the operation of the front and rear lights, brake lights and indicators, including hazard lights, before you set off.
- Use road markings and cat's eyes to help you see the direction of the road ahead.
- The lights of vehicles ahead can help you see where there's a bend and when you need to reduce your speed.
- Only overtake other vehicles when you can see that it's safe to do so.

Dealing with dazzle

- Keep your speed down when you leave brightly lit areas, to allow time for your eyes to adjust.

- Leave a large enough gap between your vehicle and the one in front, so that your lights don't dazzle the other driver.

- Adjust your dashboard lights to a comfortable level, as they can cause reflections.

- If you're dazzled, slow down or stop in a safe place until your vision returns to normal. This should only take a moment.

- Use dipped headlights where there are other vehicles, to avoid dazzling their drivers.

- Don't be tempted to flash your headlights at drivers who are using full beam. It's better to encourage others to be courteous drivers by being courteous yourself.

- If you feel your anxiety levels rising, stop your vehicle in the nearest lay-by or other suitable place and take slow, deep breaths. This activates your body's relaxation response.

Driving in wet weather

It's a Friday night and you're driving home after a hard week at work. The traffic is heavy and stormy weather conditions are making this a very difficult journey. You think other people are driving too fast and you're feeling out of your depth.

Ask yourself

- Are you accurately assessing the risk of driving in the rain? Do the wet road and spray from other vehicles mean that your ability to drive safely is affected?

- What's going through your mind? Is your desire to get home and out of the rain making you more anxious?

Strategies for safer driving

- Remind yourself that you've driven in these kinds of conditions many times before and always returned home safely.

- Use dipped headlights so that other drivers can see you.

- Keep your speed down. Windscreen wipers struggle to cope with very heavy rain, so your view of the road ahead won't be as good as it could be. Driving at a lower speed will give you more time to react to hazards that aren't immediately visible through the rain.

- Make sure that you keep the windscreen free of smears and streaks and always keep your washer bottle topped up.

- Wet weather reduces your tyres' grip on the road. Allow at least double the separation distance between you and the vehicle in front.

- If things are getting too much for you, pull over in a safe place and wait for the traffic to die down. It will be much easier to continue your drive when the roads are quieter.

- While you're waiting, do something different to help yourself relax. For example, buy a cup of coffee and read a newspaper. Enjoy some time to yourself.

Driving in snow and ice

It's been snowing and you have to make an essential journey. There are a couple of inches of snow on the roads and with every car that passes, slush is thrown up onto your car. The slush is turning to ice around the edges of your windscreen.

Suddenly you feel your tyres lose grip as you take a corner and slide a little towards the centre of the road. Around the bend, your wheels hit a rut in the snow and you find it difficult to steer. You start to feel worried about driving in these conditions.

Ask yourself

- How can you drive more safely in snow and ice?

- What can you do to minimise your risk when driving in slippery conditions?

Strategies for safer driving

- Firstly, consider whether your journey is really necessary. Can you cancel your arrangements and drive when the roads are safer?

- If you must drive in snow and ice, make sure you keep your speed down.

- Controlling a skid can be very difficult, so drive gently to avoid getting into one in the first place. Choose as high a gear as possible and avoid harsh use of the steering, brakes or accelerator.

- Be especially careful on corners and bends, where there's a greater risk of your tyres losing grip – particularly if you're driving too fast.

- Increase your following distance in icy conditions. Remember that the stopping distance in these conditions can be ten times as long as it would be in good driving conditions.

- Regularly check that your tyres have a good depth of tread and are inflated to the right pressure. Any shortcomings will be more apparent in slippery conditions.

- Make sure you have plenty of winter screen wash in your windscreen-washer bottle before you start driving.

- Remain vigilant for hazards that occur in snow and ice. Other road users may be struggling. This is especially true of large vehicles, whose wide tyres don't grip well on snow and ice.

- Be aware that there may be potholes under the snow and slush.

Parking

You're on a busy high street and are looking for somewhere to park. You spot a place and indicate to alert other road users that you're pulling into the space. As you slow down and drive past the space so that you can reverse in, it becomes clear that the space isn't as big as you thought it was.

You position your car and start reversing. The parking sensors come on and you start to feel anxious as you realise that you're not in the right position to get into the space safely. It means that the waiting traffic will have to wait even longer.

Ask yourself

- How can you prepare yourself to carry out a safe parking manoeuvre in this situation?

- What can you do to control your feelings of anxiety about parking?

Strategies for safer driving

- It isn't a good idea to rely solely on parking sensors; always use your own observation skills.

- Look in all directions continuously when reversing. Use your mirrors and turn around in your seat to look out of the windows.

- Moving slowly allows you greater control in a small space. If you move the vehicle slowly and steer quickly, you can manoeuvre the vehicle more effectively. Once you start turning into the space, coordinate your controls to keep the vehicle moving at a slow speed.

- Don't worry about holding up other road users. Focus on safely executing the parking manoeuvre.

- Remember that everyone makes mistakes sometimes.

- Don't underestimate the value of allowing extra time for finding a space and parking.

- If you feel you need to develop your parking skills, practise on your own on a quiet street or contact an ADI.

Driving near motorcyclists and cyclists

You approach a junction and look for a safe gap in the traffic on the main road before you pull out. You see a gap coming up in the traffic to the left and quickly check the traffic to the right. You're about to emerge, when at the last second, you slam on your brakes. A motorcyclist is right in front of and you didn't see her at all. Another second and you would have knocked her over.

Ask yourself

- How can you make sure you spot vulnerable road users in good time?
- What do you need to bear in mind when emerging from a junction?

Strategies for safer driving

- Make sure you fully observe the traffic, in both directions. The commonest cause of a collision with a motorcyclist or cyclist is when the driver fails to look properly. This may be because riders are smaller and therefore more difficult to see, or because there are fewer of them in traffic and you're not expecting them.

- Remember that you can't accurately judge the speed or distance of oncoming motorcyclists and cyclists unless you look at them for long enough. This may be several seconds.

- Look well into the distance to spot motorcyclists, who may be difficult to see.

- Be aware that motorcyclists and cyclists may look at you, but this isn't the same as them expecting you to emerge from the junction. Just because you've made eye contact with them does **not** mean it's safe to emerge.

- To make a safe decision about whether to emerge, you need to fully realise what you're looking at. Some drivers 'look but fail to see' oncoming motorcycles and make a decision to pull out on the basis of what seems to be an empty road.

- Cyclists can sometimes be in your blind spot at junctions, so make sure you take good all-round observation before turning.

- Allow cyclists plenty of space before you turn.

⊕ Driving offences

With experience, your ability to anticipate what might happen becomes automatic and less effort is required to process information. While it's good to develop greater confidence in your driving ability, it can have negative effects if you become too relaxed and feel that you can get away with breaking the law.

The most common driving offences include speeding, using a mobile phone while driving, and going through red lights. You may not have thought about doing any of these immediately after passing your driving test, but as time has worn on you may have felt justified in breaking the rules occasionally. Although these offences aren't always intended (speeding, for example, may be due to a lapse in concentration), most of the time they're deliberate, conscious actions.

Ask yourself what's at stake if you're caught committing a traffic offence. Which of these aspects are most important to you?

- I want to avoid getting penalty points on my driving licence.
- I want to avoid being fined.
- I want to avoid the effects of a traffic offence on my car insurance premium or my job.
- I want to avoid being involved in a collision.

Think about these consequences the next time you find yourself about to break the rules of the road.

Driving after a traffic conviction

Think about why you decided to break the law. Was there something different going on that day that made you feel justified in taking a risk? Do you regularly break the rules of the road?

Consider whether your driving style is due to certain habits that you can break, or due to your perception of risk. If you've read the previous sections of this book, you may now have a different understanding of these factors.

Strategies for safer driving

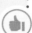

- Be aware that road safety is your first priority.
- Be aware that you have the same chance of being caught as anyone else.
- Think about the potential consequences of your actions.
- Don't get upset or angry about minor things. Accept that other road users get it wrong sometimes.
- Give yourself plenty of time for your journey, so you won't be tempted to drive too fast or jump the traffic lights.
- Never use a mobile phone while driving, even hands-free. It can distract you from the road environment and cause you to miss important information.
- Read road signs carefully and make sure you know what the rules are. If you need to refresh your knowledge, take a look at The Highway Code.
- Make sure you're fit to drive. Never drive if you've taken drugs or if you've been drinking alcohol.
- Don't drive when you're tired. You're not only more likely to commit an offence, but also more likely to be involved in an incident.

⊕ Driving as you get older

Many people have an active lifestyle in later life and want to continue to drive in order to maintain their independence. This is to be encouraged, as continuing to drive is associated with healthy ageing and general wellbeing.

Even though older drivers tend to have safer attitudes to driving and commit significantly fewer traffic offences than other age groups, some age-related deterioration in driving ability is inevitable for all of us. Only you know whether the changes in your driving ability are due to the effects of ageing or poor health, or whether you have a lack of confidence that can be improved with the right approach.

Most older drivers tend to give up driving at about the right time. However, some older drivers stop driving prematurely through lack of confidence, and this can have a large impact on their lives. Making your own decision about when to give up driving is much better than being pressured into doing so by others.

Coping strategies for older drivers

- Drive at quieter and less congested times of the day.

- Try to avoid driving at night or in poor weather conditions.

- Give yourself plenty of time for your journey, and plan your route thoroughly before you set off.

- If you're no longer confident about performing certain manoeuvres, try to plan your journey to avoid them. For example, you could avoid taking your car into congested areas by using park-and-ride facilities.

- Make sure your car is serviced regularly.

- Think about whether your car is still suitable for the kind of driving you do. If you have a large car that's difficult to manoeuvre, consider changing to something smaller.

- Are you taking full advantage of modern technology? Automatic gearboxes and more advanced features such as parking assistance can be valuable driving aids.

- Keep yourself physically fit. This will make driving less tiring.

- Exercise your mind by taking part in mentally stimulating activities.

- Ask for feedback on your driving from people you trust, such as family members.

Test yourself

Do you agree or disagree with the following statements? Be honest!

1. I believe I can deal safely with risky situations on the road.

2. If I felt my driving was becoming unsafe, I would change my driving habits.

3. My driving skills aren't as good as they used to be.

Might you be biased in your assessment of your driving skills? Are you willing to make some changes to your driving habits? If your driving skills aren't as good as they were, follow the advice in this section. If you still feel you're struggling to cope, it might be time to seek medical advice.

Warning signs

According to the National Highway Traffic Safety Administration in the US, the following are signs that it may no longer be safe for you to drive

- forgetfulness
- unusual or excessive agitation
- confusion and disorientation
- loss of coordination and trouble with stiffness in joints
- trouble walking, swallowing or hearing
- dizziness when changing positions; tripping and falling
- shortness of breath and general fatigue
- difficulty following verbal instructions and/or giving inappropriate responses to those instructions.

Additional tips to increase older driver safety

The US-based Center for Disease Control and Prevention offers this advice to older drivers

- Exercise to improve strength and flexibility.
- Ask your doctor or pharmacist to review your medicine, to reduce side effects and interactions.
- Have your eyes checked once a year.
- Drive during the day and in good weather.
- Plan your route before you drive.
- Leave an appropriate distance between yourself and the car in front of you.
- Avoid distractions inside the car.
- Consider alternatives to driving, such as using public transport or riding as a passenger with friends or family.

⊙ Improving your reaction to stress

When we rise to a challenge and succeed, we feel better about ourselves. Similarly, if you can overcome your worries and build your confidence in driving, then it will increase your self-esteem as a driver. Everyone can feel anxious, worried and stressed while driving at one time or another. These kinds of reactions can be due to the traffic or road environment as well as what's going on in your life at the time. Quite simply, you'll drive better if you develop good coping strategies to manage the demands of driving.

Think about the following approaches to dealing with driver stress.

Poor approaches

1. Confrontation – you antagonise other drivers by flashing your headlights or using the horn in anger to let them know they were at fault. You tend to want to show other drivers what you think of them.

2. Driving concerns – you have a tendency to be critical of yourself and worry about your shortcomings as a driver. You tend to blame yourself for getting too emotional or upset while driving.

3. Avoidance – your attention span is reduced to avoid dealing with the demands of driving. You may refuse to believe that anything unpleasant is going on and carry on as if nothing had happened.

Good approaches

4. Task focus – you tend to cope with the demands of driving by making a special effort to look out for hazards. You observe, anticipate and act in good time when you meet a difficult traffic situation or encounter bad weather.

5. Reappraisal – you have positive thoughts about your driving and look on the challenges you meet as useful experience. You tend to think about the benefits you gain, such as becoming a more experienced driver.

From the list above, task focus and reappraisal are the most effective strategies and should form the basis of your mental approach to driving. Confrontation and driving concerns are particularly ineffective because they're linked with negative and impaired driving behaviour. For example, confrontation is associated with committing traffic offences and making driving errors, while driving concerns is associated with self-criticism and driving errors.

> **REMEMBER** You can be a better driver by developing task-focus and reappraisal coping strategies.

Assessing your coping strategies

Ask yourself which of the following strategies you've adopted on recent journeys and assess your general approach to dealing with stress.

Poor strategies
When driving is difficult

1. I relieve my feelings by taking risks or driving fast
2. I try to make other drivers more aware of me by driving close behind them
3. I show other drivers what I think of them
4. I swear at other drivers (aloud or silently)
5. I let other drivers know they're at fault
6. I flash the headlights or use the horn in anger
7. I blame myself for getting too emotional or upset
8. I worry about what I'm going to do next
9. I worry about my shortcomings as a driver.

Good strategies
When driving is difficult

1. I try to gain something worthwhile from the drive
2. I don't let myself become distracted
3. I feel that I'm becoming a more experienced driver
4. I make an effort to stay calm and relaxed
5. I make a special effort to look out for hazards
6. I concentrate hard on what I have to do next
7. I look on the drive as useful experience
8. I think about the benefits I'll get from making the journey
9. I learn from my mistakes.

Do you mostly use good or poor coping strategies? Try to focus on increasing your use of good coping strategies and reduce your use of poor coping strategies.

⊕ Summary

In this section you've

- seen that anxiety has a negative effect on your driving performance but there are ways to reduce your nervousness and improve your confidence
- learned some strategies to help you manage the demands of difficult driving situations
- considered how you can stay safe on the road by focusing on the consequences of your actions
- reflected on the effects of ageing on driving performance, and explored some strategies to reduce your exposure to unnecessary risk and drive for longer
- examined your reaction to stress while driving, and learned better ways of coping with it.

Section four

⊙ Refresh your knowledge

In this section you'll learn

- how the UK's road environment has changed over the years
- about speed limits and rules of the road
- the procedures to follow when driving on a motorway
- how to keep your vehicle roadworthy
- what to do in the event of an emergency.

⊕ The changing road environment

There's a common misconception that Britain's roads are getting more and more dangerous. In fact, the annual number of road deaths has stayed about the same since 2010. In 2018, there were 1,784 reported road deaths in Great Britain. This is despite the fact that there was four times as much traffic on the road as there was in 1960. Developments in road engineering, legislative efforts, driver education and changes to licensing procedures have seen the UK maintain its position as one of the safest countries in which to drive.

The driving timeline

The driving test was first introduced in 1935 to help bring down the number of road-related deaths. Take a look at this timeline showing the changes to driving since 1965 and ask yourself what has changed since you passed your test.

Experimental speed limit of 70 mph imposed on motorways	**1965**	Driver and Vehicle Licensing Centre set up in Swansea
The breathalyser laws are introduced	**1967**	70 mph speed limit becomes permanent
	1970	Over 1 billion vehicle miles driven on UK roads. Over £2.5bn investment in UK roads
	1971	Number of registered vehicles reaches 19 million

1973 Crash helmets become compulsory for motorcyclists

1976 Full driving licences become valid to age 70

1978 The Highway Code introduces the Green Cross Code for pedestrians

1981 Road deaths fall below 6000 per year

1983 Front seat belt law introduced

1988 'North report' published, leading the way for the introduction of the National Driver Offender Retraining Scheme (NDORS), based on the principle that education rather than punishment may improve driver safety

Over 2 billion vehicle miles driven on UK roads

1990 Over £2 billion investment in UK roads

1991 Fixed speed cameras first appear on UK roads

Driving theory test introduced

1992 The police set up NDORS as an option for minor moving traffic offences

Full rear seat belt law introduced

Road deaths fall below 5000 per year

1996

1997 New drivers automatically disqualified and required to retake the theory and practical tests if they accrue six penalty points within the first two years after obtaining a full driving licence

1998 Road deaths fall below 3500 per year

2002 — Hazard perception test introduced

2003 — New law prohibits the use of hand-held mobile phones while driving

2007 — Number of registered vehicles reaches 31 million

Road deaths fall below 3000 for the first time since records began in 1926

2010 — 'Independent driving' element introduced to the driving test: candidates must follow road signs and make their own driving decisions for 10 minutes

2011 — 770,000 people complete the NDORS speed awareness course

2012 — 300 billion vehicle miles driven on UK roads

2013 — Road deaths reach an all-time low of 1713

2014 — Traffic on UK motorways reaches an all-time high of 64.3 billion miles travelled

2015 — The driving test is 80 years old

2017 — Changes to the driving test, introducing a longer period of independent driving and use of sat-navs

2018 — Learner drivers allowed to practise on motorways

As you can see, the past 50 years have seen major changes to the driving environment and the driver licensing process. Watch DVSA's 'Driving tests: guides for learners' videos and ask yourself how the test has changed since you passed it. Do you think you would still pass today's test? What bad habits have you developed since you gained your licence?

youtube.com/dvsagovuk

The three Es

As the timeline suggests, the road environment in the UK is constantly being influenced by

- changes in the law
- changes in the way that roads and vehicles are constructed
- changes in driver education.

Collectively, these are known in road safety as the 'three Es': engineering, education and enforcement. It's these three factors, more than any others, that have helped to bring about dramatic reductions in the road casualty rate.

Advances in driver education and enforcement

Since the driving test was first introduced in 1935, the government and local councils have tried to raise awareness of the importance of good decision-making and hazard perception, taking into account factors such as the environment, the purpose of the journey, and the personal characteristics of the individual and other drivers.

Education – often acting on the back of legislation (for example, the breathalyser laws in 1967 and the seat belt laws in 1983) – has helped to shift the focus from mechanical skills. It has brought wider recognition of the value of understanding the human aspects of driving as part of a strategy for safe driving for life.

Enforcement of traffic laws has also made a real contribution to advances in driver education and road safety.

- The introduction of fixed roadside safety cameras in 1992 resulted in a substantial reduction in speeds – and the corresponding number of incidents – when fitted at speeding black spots.

- Driver offender programmes have led to the re-education of millions of drivers who have committed driving offences such as speeding, not wearing a seat belt or careless driving. They've been supported by regular government safety awareness campaigns and police enforcement programmes.

Have you received any further driver training or education since passing your driving test?

How do you think your driving has changed since you learned to drive?

About 80% of drivers believe they're better than the average driver. What does this suggest?

⊕ Speed limits

In the early part of the 20th century, speed limits were introduced, revised and scrapped on a regular basis. By the time the national motorway speed limit was introduced in 1965, the basic structure of speed limits was established and it remains in place to this day.

You should always keep in mind that the speed limit is the absolute maximum. It doesn't mean that it's safe to drive at this speed.

National speed limits

National speed limits vary according to the type of vehicle you're driving. Unless road signs say otherwise, the standard national limits are as follows:

Type of vehicle	Built-up areas mph (km/h)	Single carriage-ways mph (km/h)	Dual carriage-ways mph (km/h)	Motorways mph (km/h)
Cars, motorcycles, car-derived vans and dual-purpose vehicles	**30** (48)	**60** (96)	**70** (112)	**70** (112)
Cars, motorcycles, car-derived vans and dual-purpose vehicles when towing caravans or trailers	**30** (48)	**50** (80)	**60** (96)	**60** (96)
Motorhomes or motor caravans (not more than 3.05 tonnes maximum unladen weight)	**30** (48)	**60** (96)	**70** (112)	**70** (112)
Motorhomes or motor caravans (more than 3.05 tonnes maximum unladen weight)	**30** (48)	**50** (80)	**60** (96)	**70** (112)
Buses, coaches and minibuses (not more than 12 metres overall length)	**30** (48)	**50** (80)	**60** (96)	**70** (112)
Buses, coaches and minibuses (more than 12 metres overall length)	**30** (48)	**50** (80)	**60** (96)	**60** (96)

Type of vehicle	Built-up areas mph (km/h)	Single carriage-ways mph (km/h)	Dual carriage-ways mph (km/h)	Motorways mph (km/h)
Goods vehicles (not more than 7.5 tonnes maximum laden weight)	**30** (48)	**50** (80)	**60** (96)	**70** (112) **60** (96) if articulated or towing a trailer
Goods vehicles (more than 7.5 tonnes maximum laden weight) in England and Wales	**30** (48)	**50** (80)	**60** (96)	**60** (96)
Goods vehicles (more than 7.5 tonnes maximum laden weight) in Scotland	**30** (48)	**40** (64)	**50** (80)	**60** (96)

REMEMBER Where no other limit is shown, the national speed limit for cars and motorcycles is

- 60 mph (96 km/h) on a single carriageway
- 70 mph (112 km/h) on a dual carriageway or motorway.

The national speed limit sign

Large vehicles on motorways

If a motorway has more than two lanes, heavy vehicles are prohibited from entering the highest-numbered lane (lane 3 on a traditional three-lane motorway), but they're permitted to overtake one another in the other lanes.

Remember that it can be difficult for drivers of large goods vehicles (LGVs) to see you, because smaller vehicles can sometimes be hidden in their blind spots. This is especially true of left-hand-drive LGVs, so scanning the road for an indication that they're about to pull out is essential.

You should follow this advice

- Don't speed up when an LGV is passing you. Instead, give the driver room to pass safely, as this will get you out of their blind spot faster.

- If an LGV is signalling to change lanes, give it space. An average LGV travelling at motorway speeds needs an eight-second gap to change lanes.

- If you're alongside or approaching a large vehicle with a view to passing it, and you see its indicator flash, prepare to move out to the next overtaking lane as soon as it's safe to do so.

- LGVs can become unstable in side winds. Keep both hands on the steering wheel when you pass an LGV or when an LGV passes you.

REMEMBER Try to avoid sitting alongside any vehicle for an extended period while overtaking.

Smart motorways

Smart motorways are monitored and controlled by new technological systems, most commonly traffic flow cameras and electronic signs on gantries above the carriageway – one for each lane. There are three main categories of smart motorway

- controlled motorways – these use variable speed limits to maintain the flow of traffic at busy times or in the event of a delay further along the motorway

- hard-shoulder running – these bring the hard shoulder into use as another lane for traffic when demand on the main lanes is high. There are refuge points at intervals alongside the motorway, to be used if your vehicle breaks down

- all-lane running – these stretches of motorway are designed without a hard shoulder. Instead, there are refuge points at intervals alongside the motorway.

Have you ever driven on a smart motorway?

Do you know what to do if you break down on a smart motorway?

For more information about smart motorways, see this website.

www.gov.uk/guidance/how-to-drive-on-a-smart-motorway

If you're driving on a smart motorway and your vehicle develops a problem, you should try to leave at the next exit or pull into a motorway service area. If you can't leave the motorway, then you should stop in one of the emergency refuge areas, where you'll be able to call for help using the roadside telephone.

If it isn't possible to do any of these things, try to get your vehicle off the carriageway and onto the verge or hard shoulder – if one is available.

⊕ Vehicle maintenance and breakdowns

You can reduce the chances of your car breaking down with preventive maintenance. Make sure that your vehicle is serviced at the recommended intervals and carry out some simple checks yourself (see below) on a regular basis. Modern cars are very reliable, but being prepared (by joining a breakdown service, for example) and knowing what to do in the event of an emergency will help to increase your confidence in driving.

Is your vehicle ready for your journey?

Just a few checks before you set off, in addition to general vehicle maintenance throughout the year, should make a breakdown unlikely.

Before you use your car, check that

- your fuel tank is full enough for your intended journey. Remember that driving at higher speeds will use more fuel – and there can sometimes be quite a distance between service areas on motorways. Allowing your fuel to run too low can cause running problems and even damage the engine

- the windscreen, windows and mirrors are clean

- all lights (including brake lights and indicators) are working. Replace any dead bulbs immediately. (It's a good idea to carry spare bulbs and fuses.) If you don't feel confident about doing this, your garage should be able to help

- the brakes are working properly. Don't drive with faulty brakes.

Check the following levels before you use the vehicle, following your car manufacturer's advice. Contact your garage if you have any concerns about the

- engine oil
- water in the radiator or expansion tank
- brake fluid
- water in the windscreen and rear-window washer bottles.

Check your tyres and make sure they're legal. They must have at least the legally specified minimum depth of tread and be free of dangerous cuts and defects. They must also be inflated to the right pressure.

Having your vehicle serviced at the recommended intervals will help to keep your vehicle reliable and prolong its life. Many modern vehicles will tell the driver when they require a service.

What to do in an emergency

Punctures and blow-outs (burst tyres)

If your car suddenly becomes unstable or you begin to notice steering problems, you might have a puncture or a blow-out. Try to stay calm and follow these steps.

- Don't brake suddenly.
- Take your foot off the accelerator.
- Try to keep a straight course by holding the steering wheel firmly.
- Get the vehicle away from the traffic (onto the hard shoulder if you're on a motorway).
- If you have to move the vehicle, do so very slowly to avoid further damage to the tyre or wheel rim.

- On a motorway, never attempt to change a wheel yourself. Always use one of the emergency telephones to call for help.

- On all other roads, get the vehicle to a place of safety. Before attempting repairs or changing a wheel, put on something to help passing drivers see you, such as a fluorescent jacket. At night or in poor visibility, a reflective garment is recommended.

Falling loads

If you're driving on a motorway and you see something fall from another vehicle, or if anything falls from your own vehicle, stop at the next emergency telephone and report the hazard. Don't try to retrieve the item yourself.

Vehicle fires

If your vehicle catches fire while you're driving, pull up as quickly and safely as possible. Get yourself and any passengers out and away from the vehicle. Then call the fire brigade. If the fire is under the bonnet, don't open the bonnet, as this will make the fire worse. If it's a small fire elsewhere, consider dousing it with a fire extinguisher, but avoid taking any risks.

Traffic incidents

If you're involved in a road traffic incident, you should stop whether or not it was your fault if

- another vehicle has been damaged

- someone else's property has been damaged

- someone other than yourself has been injured

- an animal that was either in another vehicle involved in the incident or in the road has been injured

- an item of street furniture – such as a sign or a lamp – has been damaged.

If you have to stop, you must give your name and address (and the name and address of the vehicle's legal owner if the car isn't yours) and the registration number of the vehicle to anybody who was involved in the incident. You should also ask for the same information from any other driver(s)/persons who are affected. If you don't exchange these details at the time of the incident, you should report them to the police as soon as possible (immediately in Northern Ireland) and in any case within 24 hours.

If you break down

In the event of a breakdown

- Activate your hazard warning lights.
- Get the vehicle as far off the road as possible.
- Put on a high-visibility jacket.
- Place a warning triangle on the road, well back from the car. Note: never do this on a motorway, because it's too dangerous.

- Contact a garage or breakdown service and wait in a safe place, away from the car, for them to arrive.

On a motorway

If you break down on a motorway, steer your vehicle onto the hard shoulder as far to the left as you can, away from the traffic. When you stop, it's a good idea to turn your wheels slightly to the left, so your vehicle isn't pushed onto the main carriageway if it's hit from behind.

You should also be aware of the following procedures

- Switch on your hazard lights to warn other drivers that you've broken down.
- Make sure your sidelights are on in poor visibility or at night.
- Don't open the offside (driver's side) doors.
- Warn your passengers of the dangers of passing vehicles.
- Keep animals inside the vehicle.
- Along with your passengers, leave the vehicle by the nearside (passenger side) doors, away from the traffic. Lock all doors, except the front passenger door.
- Telephone the emergency services.
- Wait on the embankment at the other side of the crash barrier, away from the hard shoulder.

On a level crossing

If you break down on a level crossing, get everyone out of the vehicle and clear of the crossing immediately. Call the signal operator from the phone provided. Only move your vehicle if the operator tells you to do so.

For more information on what to do if you break down, see section 15 of *The Official DVSA Guide to Driving – the essential skills* or the eBook *Breakdowns and Incidents,* from the DVSA Safe Driving for Life Series.

⊕ Summary

In this section you've

- reviewed the key milestones in the development of the UK road environment
- checked your knowledge of national and local speed limits, and considered the consequences of an inappropriate choice of speed
- reflected on the way you drive on motorways and learned some techniques for safer use of these roads
- seen how to reduce the chances of a breakdown and what to do in an emergency.

For more help and advice on developing your hazard perception skills, see *The Official DVSA Guide to Hazard Perception DVD-ROM* and *The Official DVSA Guide to Driving – the essential skills.*

Take a free practice theory test, and a road signs quiz, at this website.

safedrivingforlife.info

Further driver training

Throughout this book, we've suggested that taking lessons with an approved driving instructor (ADI) may help you to refresh your skills and get some practical guidance behind the wheel.

Some ADIs have received specialist training on the human factors in driving and have developed their ability to address many of the concerns you may have about your driving, in a practical one-to-one environment. This is referred to as client-centred learning or driver coaching.

You can find your nearest ADI on GOV.UK.

www.gov.uk/find-driving-schools-and-lessons

You can also develop your driving by getting in touch with one of the following organisations to find some advanced training that suits your needs.

The AA

Go to **http://www.theaa.com/driving-school/qualified-driver-lessons** or call **0330 100 7474.**

Whether you've just passed or are more experienced, book refresher qualified driver lessons to practise any driving skills (general, town driving, all-weather driving, out-of-town driving and rural roads, night driving, dual carriageways, motorway driving). If you're a new driver, take the six-hour Pass Plus course to gain confidence and experience on the roads.

DIAmond Advanced Motorists

Go to **driving.org/advanced-training** or call **020 8686 8010.**

A DIAmond Advanced Instructor can familiarise you with the requirements of the test and give you feedback to work on. The hour-long test is objectively scored, going beyond style and technique to reflect a commitment to driving in a way that saves fuel, minimises wear and tear, and stresses forward planning and anticipation. No special techniques are needed, but fuel-efficient driving means gentle acceleration, avoiding jerky car control and planning manoeuvres well in advance.

IAM RoadSmart (formerly the Institute of Advanced Motorists)

Go to **iamroadsmart.com/local-groups** and enter your postcode for your local group or call **0300 303 1134.**

The advanced driver courses provide you with everything you need to pass the advanced driving test, and when you pass you'll become a full member of IAM RoadSmart. There are over 200 local volunteer groups and yours will support you in preparing for the test. Included in the fee is 12 months' membership of IAM RoadSmart and *RoadSmart*, the members-only magazine.

Royal Society for the Prevention of Accidents (RoSPA)

Go to **rospa.com/safety-training/on-road/driver-training/experienced**

RoSPA's Experienced Driver Assessment is designed for peace of mind. A qualified Police Advanced Driver will assess your driving over one hour, and give you a verbal and written assessment, as well as your certificate of completion. This is designed to help you make an informed decision as to whether or not to do further advanced training.

Changing your driving behaviour

Throughout this book, we've seen that improving your driving judgement, knowledge and skills starts with increasing your awareness of the human factors that affect the way you drive. As a final exercise, think about the following process of behavioural change and try to work out which stage you're at. Each stage will have its own difficulties and obstacles to overcome, but with a little time, effort and application, you'll find that your driving confidence really can improve.

Stage 1:   **Precontemplation (Not ready to change)**

You're unaware that your behaviour is problematic, and you're not thinking about making any change.

Think about accessing information from reliable sources to increase your awareness of what's at stake.

Stage 2:   **Contemplation (Getting ready)**

You're beginning to recognise that something needs to change to improve your driving behaviour. You look at the pros and cons involved.

You've read this book. Now think about what's at stake if you don't make a change, and what you can gain if you do make a change.

Stage 3:   **Preparation (Ready to change)**

You intend to take action to improve your driving, and you may begin to take small steps towards a change.

Think about the advice contained in this book and develop some manageable goals over the next few weeks. Don't try to do too much at once; instead, take small steps towards your ultimate goal. Develop an action plan to help you achieve it.

Stage 4:   **Taking action**

You're making specific modifications to your behaviour, and you're learning new and safer ways of driving.

You're now implementing your action plan. Don't be put off if it takes a little time to see an improvement in your driving. Keep trying. Think about how you need to build on your successes; notice even small improvements and congratulate yourself on them.

Stage 5: **Maintenance**

You've been able to see a steady improvement over time, and you're focused on making sure you keep it up.

If you have a bad day and return to your old ways, don't be disheartened. Refocus and move on. You know you can do it. Think about how you can continue to improve by selecting and working on different aspects of your driving. It's time to think about a new set of goals.

REMEMBER You can meet the challenge of changing your driving behaviour and improving your driving abilities if you believe you can. Imagine how good you'll feel when you're driving better. With the right motivation and a bit of persistence, you'll be surprised by how much you can achieve in a short space of time.

⊕ Photographic credits

Section one

Page 1 – Man looking in rear-view mirror
George Doyle/Stockbyte/Thinkstock

Page 8 – Think! emoticons road safety poster
Think! Road Safety/Department for Transport

Page 31 – Car on rural road
Highways England

Section two

Page 52 – Family in car
Mark Bowden/iStock/Thinkstock

Page 60 – Think! Drug driving poster
Think! Road Safety/Department for Transport

Page 69 – Road widening
Highways England

Page 69 – Tunnel
Highways England

Page 70 – Shared space Kensington
Chris Marshall/CBRD

Section three

Page 82 – Child in car seat with teddy
Jupiterimages/BananaStock/Thinkstock

Page 85 – Motorway at dusk
Krzysztof Melech/iStock/Thinkstock

Page 86 – Cars driving on motorway in wet weather
Highways England

Page 91 – Traffic light
Jupiterimages/Polka Dot/Thinkstock

Page 91 – Speed camera
Ashley Pickering/iStock/Thinkstock

Section four

⊕ Appendix: The national standard for driving

The national standard for driving describes the skills, knowledge and understanding you need to be a safe and responsible driver of a car or light van.

Based on extensive research and consultation, the standard is the basis for the driving test and all the official learning materials that DVSA publishes for drivers, at every stage of their driving career.

The standard is split into five sections, or 'roles', and each role covers a different aspect of driving a car or light van.

Each of these roles is then broken down into units, which cover specific areas within each role.

The units are further broken down into elements, which cover

* what you must be able to do
* what you must know and understand.

The full national standard can be found at **www.gov.uk**, but the following table sets out

* the five roles
* their units
* an example of an element and what you'll need to know and understand in that element.

Role 1	Prepare yourself, the vehicle and its passengers for a journey
Unit 1.1	Prepare yourself and passengers for a journey
	Element 1.1.2 Make sure you're fit to drive
	You must be able to assess whether your ability to drive safely and legally is affected by your emotional state, a short- or long-term physical condition, or tiredness.
	You must know and understand what the law says about driving while you have illegal or controlled substances or alcohol in your system.
Unit 1.2	Make sure the vehicle is roadworthy
Unit 1.3	Plan a journey
Role 2	Guide and control the vehicle
Unit 2.1	Start, move off, stop and leave the vehicle safely and responsibly
Unit 2.2	Drive the vehicle safely and responsibly
	Element 2.2.4 Steer the vehicle safely
	You must be able to steer the vehicle safely and responsibly in all road and traffic conditions.
	You must know and understand how to keep safe control of the steering wheel.
Unit 2.3	Drive the vehicle while towing a trailer or caravan
Role 3	Use the road in accordance with The Highway Code
Unit 3.1	Negotiate the road correctly
	Element 3.1.4 Drive on motorways and dual carriageways
	You must be able to drive in the most suitable lane.
	You must know and understand that you may not stop on a motorway except in an emergency.
Unit 3.2	Comply with signals, signs and road markings

⊕ Index

Learning to drive, ride or simply want to brush up on your knowledge?

- All the latest revision questions and answers
- Over 100 high-quality hazard perception clips
- Accessible on any internet-connected device

Visit **www.dvsalearningzone.co.uk** and enter code **SD10** to save 10%.